THREE CENTURIES OF FRENCH ART

THREE CENTURIES OF FRENCH ART

Edited with an Introductory Essay by F. Lanier Graham

Selections from
The Norton Simon, Inc. Museum of Art
and The Norton Simon Foundation

THE FINE ARTS MUSEUMS OF SAN FRANCISCO:
CALIFORNIA PALACE OF THE LEGION OF HONOR

Exhibited at the California Palace of the Legion of Honor
beginning May 3, 1973

Copyright © 1973 by The Fine Arts Museums of San Francisco
ISBN 0-88401-001-5
Library of Congress Catalogue Card No. 73-76081

Designed and produced by Adrian Wilson
Composed by Mackenzie & Harris, Inc. in Centaur and Arrighi types
Printed by the Recorder-Sunset Press

Contents

Alphabetical List of
Catalogue & Plate Numbers

Preface

Norton Simon has taken a far-sighted look at that recent phenomenon in American art museums described as the "edifice complex," backed off, and developed instead an imaginative plan for utilizing the extraordinary collections of the corporately supported Norton Simon, Inc. Museum of Art and the previously established Norton Simon Foundation. The plan is going a long way to balance, both geographically and programmatically, the artistic resources of the United States.

He reasons that although it may cost only several million dollars to construct a new museum, it would cost a million or more each year to operate a museum adequate to house those collections. The money which might be spent on structure and tied up forever in operating costs can better be spent on acquiring great works of art.

Mr. Simon understands that a sufficient number of art museums may already exist in this country, and that the real need is for more masterpieces to make each one more meaningful. The innovative plan is to present carefully selected portions of the collections in existing museums for an extended period, at least a year and perhaps longer.

From an incomparable wealth of alternatives each museum has been able to select works of art which fill gaps in their permanent collections and enrich the opportunities of neighboring educational institutions. Thus, the Los Angeles County Museum of Art, Princeton University Art Museum, and the Houston Museum of Fine Arts have at present a broad representation of Western art since the Renaissance from various centuries and national schools. The Pasadena Art Museum, specializing in contemporary art, has at present 20th century sculpture. It is anticipated that an Indian and Southeast Asian exhibition will open in the Fall at the Metropolitan Museum of Art in New York.

This selection responds to the needs of the recently merged M. H. de Young Memorial Museum and the California Palace of the Legion of Honor. As part of a master-plan for maximizing the usefulness of the combined collections, the Trustees have decided to make the Legion of Honor the only museum in America devoted to French art. This exhibition was selected to encourage the Legion of Honor in its new direction.

Enthusiastic endorsement of the simultaneous exhibition plan comes from the Norton Simon, Inc. Board of Directors. We are grateful to them and David J. Mahoney, Chairman of the Board, for their encouragement and support. Considerable credit for articulating and implementing the plan goes to Robert S. Macfarlane, Jr., who as president of Foundation Funds of Norton Simon, Inc. is Mr. Simon's liaison with the museums. Part of his responsibility was to insure that the institutions selected to receive works of art are deepening their commitments to the communities they serve. He was able to conclude that The Fine Arts Museums of San Francisco are indeed strengthening their ties with colleges and universities in the Bay Area through a revitalized Educational Department, and are reaching out actively for wider audiences with new ideas in programming through the Art School and Docent Council.

Museum visitors are seldom aware of the months of detailed preparation required to produce an exhibition and catalogue of this scope. In this work we were assisted continually by Darryl E. Isley, Curator and Vice-President, Norton Simon, Inc. Museum of Art, and his Assistant Curator, Sara Campbell. He not only provided almost all of the photographs for research and reproduction, and most of the basic information for the catalogue entries, but also worked as an active collaborator in the process of selection with our Chief Curator, F. Lanier Graham.

Working together, we have been able to present an exceptionally rich and cohesive exhibition of French painting and sculpture. As an introduction to the "Three Centuries of French Art," we are indebted to Mr. Graham for an incisive survey of this era's history from a point of view which is long overdue.

Sincere gratitude is also due to the tireless secretarial assistance of Frances Barrett and Gloria Smith; the production co-ordination of Lynda Kefauver; the patient research of Helen K. Crotty, Marion C. Stewart and Jean Chaitin; the skillful registration of Frederic P. Snowden and Jan Heath; and the sensitive designs of Thomas H. Garver and Royal A. Basich for the installation, and Adrian Wilson for the catalogue.

And we would like to extend particular thanks to The Museum Society who made the catalogue possible; and to Mayor Joseph Alioto and the Board of Supervisors who recognized with us how important an exhibition of this quality is to the spiritual well-being of San Francisco.

IAN MCKIBBIN WHITE
Director of the Museums

Foreword

The Trustees of the Norton Simon, Inc. Museum of Art and The Norton Simon Foundation are pleased to have this exhibition of French art at the California Palace of the Legion of Honor. It is fitting that an exhibition of the art of France be held at the Legion. This museum, perhaps more than any other in America, has had an enduring interest in bringing French art to this country in an effort to promote better understanding between the people of the United States and France.

Our collections have been formed with the express hope of improving communication at the individual, national and international level. Art is a communication channel that can take people and open them up in a unique way. Art can start getting people to look at themselves which is important since one of the prime problems in society is the need for introspection. Art can help us not only look at ourselves, but also it makes it possible to see others with greater sensitivity and insight. It is particularly useful when cultural barriers are involved. The more we are exposed to the art of other countries, the better we are able to understand and communicate with the people from whose culture the art comes.

Over the years we have been fortunate to bring together and exhibit a wide ranging selection of paintings, sculpture, prints and drawings from Europe with whom America traditionally has had the closest ties. And now that the conflict in Southeast Asia appears near an end, we feel it important that the people of this country are able to relate more completely with the people who live in that too little understood part of the world. Therefore we have enlarged our focus and recently embarked on a program to collect and exhibit the art of India and Southeast Asia.

Communication and education are the basic philosophical principles that guide our plans. We have inaugurated a program of making available selections from our collections on something of a rotating basis to various parts of the country. In each of these locations we have encouraged the museum to work closely not only with the general community but particularly with nearby educational institutions. We are hopeful that the present loan will be helpful in the teaching programs of the many fine grade schools, high schools, colleges and universities in the Bay Area during the next year. The purposes of the Norton Simon, Inc. Museum of Art and The Norton Simon Foundation will have been well served if human understanding and communication is strengthened through this exhibition.

NORTON SIMON
President
Norton Simon, Inc. Museum of Art
and The Norton Simon Foundation

Traditions and Revolutions: An Introduction to the History of French Painting and Sculpture

Facts require interpretation; pictures need no spokesman. The problem is not so much to fit them into an arbitrary system of classification as to place them in as clear a light as possible.

JACQUES THUILLIER

A curious, if logical, corollary of our modern concern for the purely formal qualities of art has been to deny the significance of "message" morality and the social correlatives of past art, but if we were to set aside the social history of . . . France, we could not understand its art. . . . A study of the visual arts alone could not possibly explain the pulling together of so many diverse currents. . . . While we should avoid the view that art mirrors society (only bad art does), we must understand that it interacts with social currents.

ROBERT L. HERBERT

Arts and artifacts from the 18th, 20th, or any other century, cannot be understood in terms of particular forms alone. Nor is it enough merely to refer to their having an "historical background" or to set them in some "historical context." The history must come first.

One sees art and artifacts as responses to social need, as products of social function, with forms determined by ideology, and a whole new approach to art opens up. . . . Once realize this, and art history becomes something far more significant than the mere assembling of chronological accounts of changing personal tastes, whose internal development can be analyzed but whose motivation must remain inexplicable.

No longer "history of art," it becomes "history in art"—a study of arts and artifacts seen as records of successive ideological movements through the ages, providing a unique key to the ultimate meaning of human life . . .

ALAN GOWANS

Part One:

The Formation of Traditions

For most people who enjoy the history of French painting and sculpture, the beginnings of their interest usually date from the 17th century. For this to be true may seem surprising at first. French culture, of course, is considerably older than that. The origins of French art are almost as old as the documented history of humanity. The cave paintings of Lascaux are more than 15,000 years old. But one should not think of these Stone Age artists as French, except in the most allegorical way.

It was not until the 5th century, A.D., when the Roman Empire was crumbling in the West, that the Merovingian dynasty of a "wandering tribe" called the Franks won military control over most of what Caesar knew as Gaul. At this point the political geography starts to resemble that of modern France. Then the importation of Christianity, and many other elements of Roman culture, by Clovis (481-511) and his successors through to Charlemagne (742-811), began to catalyze the primitive energy of these passionate nature-worshippers into that profound flowering of spiritual force which was the art of the Middle Ages—an art to which French artists were the principal contributors.

Architecture was the "mother art" of France for a millennium. Sculpture had no meaningful existence outside the context of a cathedral. The painter's craft was similarly subordinated, within the theological hierarchy of the Gothic Church, to the illumination of manuscripts and the fabrication of stained-glass windows. For better or worse, the medieval era is very distant from our own. It is no longer quite within our grasp. We can come no closer than to the glowing memory of a dream.

During the 14th and 15th centuries, painting and sculpture began to follow increasingly independent developments. But for all the intrinsic interest and quality of French work, the primary changes in aesthetic theory and style during this period tended to originate outside of France. By the year 1400, the Italians and the Flemish had started to lead the Western World into the Renaissance.

For the 15th and 16th centuries, the student of art history concentrates on Florence and Siena, Venice and Rome, Bruges and Brussels and Nuremberg. Paris slips back under a veil of vague recollections. This is not to suggest that important work was not being done in France. The School of Fontainebleau, which flourished under King Francis I (1515-1547) and his descendants, contains many remarkable qualities that are only beginning to be fully appreciated. The extraordinary way in which these artists fused reality and fantasy resulted in some of the most elegantly beautiful forms ever produced by Mannerism.

But the average student is more likely to remember that France invited Leonardo da Vinci, Benvenuto Cellini, Andrea del Sarto, Il Rosso and Primaticcio to visit a court that was searching for an artistic identity, rather than recall the names of Jean Fouquet (ca. 1420-1481), François Clouet (ca. 1510-1572), or Corneille de Lyon (active 1533-1574). And the average layman probably will not be able to think of the name of a single French artist before Poussin and Claude. Here then is where modern consciousness of French painting and sculpture begins. Here is where this exhibition begins. And with good reason.

SEVENTEENTH CENTURY:

Creation and Institutionalization

A fundamental change in the history of France took place in the 17th century. It was during this period that aesthetic standards were established by which all subsequent painting and sculpture would be judged. By the end of the century, Paris had replaced Rome as the political, military, economic and cultural capital of the West. And it would continue to be the nerve center of the visual arts right up until our own lifetime. The development of this extraordinary tradition is one of the richest chapters in the history of Western civilization.

The immediate successors of Francis I were not of a very high caliber. Even if they had been, they probably could have done little to prevent the bitter religious wars which kept France in turmoil throughout the second half of the 16th century. Peace was only established when the Protestant king, Henry IV (1589-1610), the first of the Bourbon dynasty, decided that "Paris is well worth a Mass" and converted to Catholicism in 1593, then granted the tolerant Edict of Nantes in 1598. He took over the leadership of Europe's most populated nation—15 million people, very few of whom even spoke a common dialect. Before his tragic assassination, he was able to lay the foundations for a prosperous and united country by significantly improving agricultural and transportation systems; developing the colonization of North American provinces; and starting to centralize political control. A state of unprecedented power was emerging.

During the reign of the ineffectual Louis XIII (1610-1643), the chief architect of that progress was Cardinal Richelieu (1585-1642). This master of organization managed to take most of the administration of national affairs away from nobility (who naturally feared a centralizing government) and place it in the hands of an efficient civil service. With this improved ability to collect taxes, Richelieu was able to build the military to a point that enabled France to become the principal winner of that bloody finale of the Reformation—the Thirty Years War of 1618-1648. From his appointment in 1624, Richelieu devoted considerable attention to the arts in a manner he felt appropriate to a great nation.

Richelieu's hand-picked successor, Mazarin (1602-1661), continued the state policy of trying to centralize all important authority by insisting on the Divine Right of Absolute Monarchy. Towards the glorification of that end, French artists were patronized as never before. The Royal Academy of Painting and Sculpture was established in 1648. Self-consciously encouraging French artists, the Royal Collection grew rapidly, and by 1709 would hold over 2,400 pictures.

By the time the Academy was founded, France had finally discovered the aesthetic center of her new selfhood, and could enter into the continuing process of exploring its spiritual depth. This change in national confidence was dramatic. Only a generation before, in the first quarter of the century, French artists were still searching for a meaningful point of departure, a definite identity. Most of the painting was being done under the fading shadow of the second School of Fontainebleau. And much of that was being executed by artists imported from Antwerp. In the early 1620s, when it came time to award the most important possible royal commission, the Life and Times of King Henry IV and Queen Marie de Médicis was given to Peter Paul Rubens. No one in France could have done anything like what Rubens did. Those who had equivalent genius were just beginning to find themselves, and they were not looking in the direction of that flamboyantly Baroque style.

French art was defining itself differently, under the inspiration of more classical restraint. During the second quarter of the 17th century, France flowered in the soil of its vastly improved economic and political system. In the provinces, the Le Nain brothers (1588-1677) and Georges de La Tour (1593-1652) cultivated the solid roots of realism, as did the "little masters" of still life in the back streets of Paris. Courtly painters like Simon Vouet (1590-1649) returned from Italy, with an expanded sense of amplitude in form and space, to plant those interacting influences of Carravaggio and the Carracci which would blossom as suitable images for the French posture of Counter Reformation. In the process, painting became the principal visual art form.

The entire nation began to center its aesthetic ideas on the brilliant rationalism of Déscartes (1596-1650), the justly proportioned architecture of Mansart (1598-1666), the measured dignity in the drama of Corneille (1606-1684), and the subtle sensuality of those lovers of ancient Attica—Perrier, Stella, Blanchard, la Hyre, Bourdon, Dughet, Le Sueur, and Le Brun—who founded their Academy in the image of that Athenian grove in which Plato met with his disciples. Most of these aesthetic qualities were articulated by Poussin [Plate 1] and Claude [Plate 2] and presented to the world as French art at its finest. Thanks to their towering genius, French painting finally became international again in its appeal and influence.

The founding of the Academy was an attempt to consolidate and perpetuate this national achievement. Its expressed purpose was to establish and maintain standards of excellence for the newly professionalized stature of the "liberal artist." Since Roman times, art, for the most part, had been regarded simply as one of the common crafts, for which the guild system of apprenticeship training was thought to be quite adequate. Now the standards of a more complex culture were being imposed. Technical skill was to be supplemented by a curriculum of history and theory. As an official arm of a very strong government, this Academy would enjoy considerably more prestige than earlier ones in other countries which were organized and perpetuated by artists.

Historians have been properly critical of the limitations that the Academy imposed on creative activity. The restrictions were indeed severe. Drawing was stressed over color. The past was emphasized over the present. Preferred subject matter was categorized. The "noble" matter of history, either classical or biblical, was valued highest over any contemporary subject, whether portraiture, landscape, scenes of everyday activity or humble still life [Plates 3 and 4]. Every school of art was given a numerical rank of merit in descending order, from the Ancients, to Raphael, Poussin, and on down to the Venetians, Flemish and Dutch.

Appropriately, it was the attitude of Poussin— the foremost French painter of the century—that was institutionalized by the Academy. The classical balance of his style, and his desire to paint historical allegories which were both intellectually satisfying and morally elevating, were to dominate the academic approach to painting for the next three centuries in Europe and America.

Unfortunately, ideals usually change in the process of institutionalization. The original spirit of the individual genius tends to get lost in the emulation of its appearance. The outward image of orderliness spreads out and tries to cover up the absence of creative activity.

It should not be surprising that the academic approach, in 17th century France and elsewhere, was rarely, if ever, responsible for the production of great art. But it should also be acknowledged that it was responsible for encouraging a great deal of good art. As an on-going environment, it was an important catalyst. It brought into being many artists when there were few. And once there were many, it was a stimulating presence to either move in the direction of, or recoil against. The very fact of its existence may help to explain why most of the countries which produced great painters during the first half of the 17th century—Holland, Flanders and Spain—were not able to generate a continuing tradition of importance in the succeeding centuries, while France did.

At its founding, the implied purpose of the

French Academy was also to contribute to the glorification of the country and its King, who was showing himself to be uniquely qualified to serve as a Divine Monarch. When Louis XIV (1643-1715) grew to maturity, and decided to assume personal control of government in 1661, the efforts of Richelieu and Mazarin had paved the way for the political doctrine of absolutism which the King and his minister, Colbert (1665-1683), would bring to its historical zenith. France was becoming the acknowledged leader of almost every field—agricultural, commercial, industrial, military, diplomatic, visual, verbal and philosophical. As the most powerful individual in Europe, the King could enjoy the privilege of believing and saying *"L'état, c'est moi"* (I am the State).

People were starting to believe that the radical idea of the Polish astronomer, Copernicus (1473-1543), was actually true: "the sun as if sitting on a royal throne, governs the family of stars which move around it." Déscartes had built his system of modern thought around the concept of an orderly whole with all the lines of force emanating from a single source. The entire socio-political structure of France was designed around similar principles, with Louis XIV at the very center. It was this idea of the *Grand Monarch* of the *Grand Nation* in its *Grand Siècle* which was given expression in the Palace of Versailles. As the King said in the process of presenting this project in 1661 to the members of the Academy: "Gentlemen, I entrust you with the most precious thing on earth, my fame."

Under the virtual dictatorship of Charles Le Brun (1619-1690), who became Director of the Academy that Colbert reorganized in 1663, all of the artistic resources of France for a generation were drawn upon in the realization of this spectacular project. Although the achievements of individual artists were less great than they had been during the first half of the century, their collective effort—in city-planning, architecture, landscape, painting, sculpture, and decorative arts—resulted in one of the most glorious achievements in the history of Europe.

The government offices moved to Versailles in 1683, and the court gradually numbered 10,000. Here the disenfranchised aristocracy were kept constantly entertained by the plays of Molière and Racine, the operas of Lully, and the *ballet de cour* in which Louis XIV, an excellent dancer, would sometimes appear in the role of Apollo. Every architectural axis, each of the innumerable social ceremonies and political intrigues were focused around the State Bedchamber of the *Roi du Soleil*, the Sun King.

The remarkable personalities of the King and those who made his system work were given lasting expression by the best portraitists of the age—Rigaud [Plate 6] and Largillière [Plate 5], who amplified the Baroque tradition established by Philippe de Champaigne. Each of these richly sensuous images is not only the delineation of a singular individual, but also an icon through which the world should see the grandiose ideals of a Divine Monarchy.

The Sun King's dreams of territorial and aesthetic power eventually almost bankrupted the nation's treasury. The limited military conquests in the first half of his reign were reluctantly accepted by the rest of Europe. But when he attempted to assimilate Spain at the turn of the century, he posed too great a threat to the "balance of power" and was stopped by a Grand Alliance of everyone else under the leadership of Marlborough. By the Treaty of Utrecht in 1713, France was firmly contained, but hardly humiliated. Both the aggressor and the counter-aggressors had exercised a classical restraint.

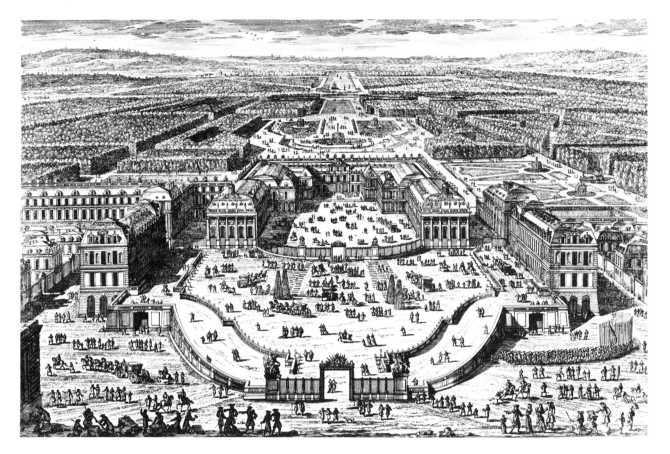

FIGURE 2: Adam Perelle, *View of Versailles.*
Engraving,
The Metropolitan Museum of Art, New York.
Rogers Fund, 1920

EIGHTEENTH CENTURY:

Rococo, Reason and Revolution

In 1715 Louis XIV's great grandson, Louis XV, succeeded as a boy of five. The aggressive spirit in the country was dead. For the first time in centuries, wars were to become relatively minor, infrequent and off French soil. For most of the 18th century, expansionism was limited to Eastern Europe. France was ready to enjoy the pleasures of peace.

A change in the cultural mood of France started to appear before the turn of the century. For most of the 17th century only men sat for portraits. But when Mignard succeeded Le Brun in 1690, he was able to start a fashion for mythological portraits of women as well. The psychology of the country was softening. An exclusively patristic principle was starting to be balanced by its matristic counterpart. A society which had worked so hard for a century to control its environment had succeeded gloriously. Now that the environment was satisfying in itself, the society did not need to strive so

aggressively for world recognition. Thought-patterns could afford to retire from the sun-drenched attitude of rigorously analytical logic to enjoy the moonlit pleasures of intuition and spontaneity.

In 1699, the aging Louis XIV himself found that some of the architectural designs being submitted to him were too ponderous. He requested more youthfulness. The Grand Manner of the authoritative Classical Baroque was over. From now on overwhelming images of massive weight and ponderous grandeur would be replaced by those of lightness and intimacy. The Rococo style of the next half century would expand human sensibility in a very different direction, attuning it to spontaneous freedom of association and more delicate shades of feeling.

During the first half of the 18th century, the court of Louis XV (1715-1774) continued to be the principal patron of French art, and the taste-makers for most of the rest of Europe from London to Moscow, between which imitations of Versailles sprang up everywhere. During this period, the courtly art of the Rococo style developed richly under the inspiration of a succession of royal mistresses—especially the powerful and extravagant Marquise de Pompadour—from 1745 until her death in 1764, when she was followed by the daughter of a Paris gatekeeper who was ennobled as Comtesse du Barry.

Watteau [Plate 7], Pater [Plate 8] and Lancret helped this audience untie itself from the anchors of historical awareness and remove the ballast of everyday reality, so that they could float suspended in a world of private dreams. During these halcyon days, their lavishly appointed rooms were filled with perfumed allegories of sensual delight by Falconet (1716-1791) and Clodion (1738-1814), Nattier (1685-1766), Boucher (1703-1770) and the most brilliant of them all—young Fragonard (1732-1806), before he retired from court into the profound poetry of his own private world [Plates 12-14].

By the middle of the century, however, the oceans of new reality were rising up around this artificial island of Feudalism's last flowering. A shifting in the nature of patronage was altering the course of art history. As William Fleming has observed: "More and more, it was now the middle class who wrote and read the books, who constructed and lived in the buildings, who painted and bought the pictures, and who composed and listened to the music."

During the Regency of the Duke of Orléans (1715-1723) the aristocracy grew tired of the constant formality required by the court etiquette of Versailles. They moved back to Paris and started to establish themselves in the smaller, more informal townhouses known as *hôtels*. In the city, the upper classes and the middle classes began to rub shoulders on the street and in the concert halls as never before. More importantly, the most sympathetic of the former and the most brilliant of the latter began to touch minds with one another in a new social institution known as the *salon*.

As Kenneth Clark has observed, "Those small social gatherings of intelligent men and women, drawn from all over Europe, who met in the rooms of gifted hostesses like Madame du Deffand and Madame Geoffrin, were for forty years the centers of European civilisation." The hostesses were neither terribly good looking nor extremely rich. In fact, a great deal of the aristocracy's capital was wiped out in the crash of 1720. People were drawn to their homes because they wanted to discuss ideas and share feelings with like-minded people. They wanted to do it not briefly and stiffly in long, cold palace corridors, nor two-dimensionally in letters or pamphlets, but in the natural human relationship of a few people sitting together at ease, through an afternoon or evening. We know a great deal about what they looked like, and thought about themselves, thanks to the incisive characterizations of Maurice Quentin de La Tour [Plate 9].

The people who gathered to talk were not the jaded effete of the *Ancien Régime*, but the finest thinkers of the time—people like Montesquieu (1689-1755), Voltaire (1694-1778), Rousseau (1712-1778) and Diderot (1713-1784). The latter eventually edited the collected wisdom of these *philosophes* (and 170 other scientists, jurists, economists, artists, educators, agriculturalists, etc.) in the great *Encyclopédie*, or *Classified Dictionary of Sciences, Arts and Trades* in 30 volumes between 1751 and 1772. This extraordinary publication became the principal vehicle for "enlightened" thought throughout the whole of the civilized world where French had become the second language.

During the 17th century's "Age of Reason" the effort of the greatest minds had been directed towards the finding of universally valid truths in every field of endeavor, from the science of Déscartes and Newton to the political "common sense" of John Locke (1632-1704). During the 18th century's "Age of Enlightenment" the effort was to spread the word of those hitherto esoteric insights and discoveries to everyone, so that they could be applied to life's daily problems.

The problems that the *philosophes* confronted in their *salons* were the most important that they could be considering. By the early 18th century, not only the very decadent institution of the Church, but Christianity itself as a source of spiritual satisfaction, creative inspiration, and operating morality had lost its persuasiveness in the minds of most intellectuals for the first time in a thousand years. They were confronted with the staggering problem of creating a new morality, a new religion. Monarchy as a political system was proving equally inadequate. They were faced with the extraordinary task of trying to generate new forms of government and justice.

Over a long and painful process, a modern form of Humanism would emerge from their collective mind. The metaphysical beauty of Nature's visual manifestations and underlying principles would be worshipped. Faith in Empirical Experience would replace faith in Revelation. Morality would be the natural outgrowth of mankind's respect and concern for one another as human beings. And Government would have to become a much more democratic process. The guide to all behavior would be Reason. With Reason man can discover the "Natural Law" by which our environment and our interpersonal relationships should be regulated. Their fundamental assumption was that humanity was not born in a state of "Original Sin," which it must work to change within itself, according to other people's directives. They looked at American Indians and Polynesian natives as assurance that humanity is born good; and that it is the corrupting influences of an evil social system that must be changed. With an unlimited quantity of optimism, they believed in the perfectability of man and the progress of the human race.

These were thoughts that led to revolutions. The *Encyclopédie* was suppressed twice before it was finally published under pressure from people who gathered in *salons*. What enabled them to have political force was the outgrowth of an interconnected network of historical developments.

In addition to invectives against social corruption and religious "superstition," there was an enormous amount of technical information in the *Encyclopédie* about fertilizers and husbandry; new ways to smelt iron, use water wheels and steam engines; how to streamline banking and insurance procedures. This kind of information had been published widely for decades before being concentrated in the *Encyclopédie*. Thousand of farmers, manufacturers and financiers had started to use this new scientific information to improve their capacity to produce goods and services. The size of meat-animals was trebling; the acre-yield of grain fields was doing even better. Fabric merchants were becoming millionaires. To keep up with this unprecedented economic explosion, paper money started to replace metal coins. The Industrial Revolution and its agricultural counterpart were well underway by mid-century.

None of this affected the peasantry very much. Their way of life remained about as it was in the Middle Ages. But the middle class, who were the principal users of the new information, had grown to such numbers and economic strength that they had to be reckoned with. They were developing their own political ideas and aesthetic sensibilities.

FIGURE 4:   Jean François de Troy, *A Reading from Molière,* ca. 1740.
Oil on canvas,
Private Collection, London.
The Bettman Archive, Inc.

Late in the 17th century the Academy itself had started to respond to newer sensibilities. There was a polarization among its members. The conservatives, called "Poussinistes," continued to insist on the primary importance of visual forms being contained within the clear outline of drawing. The progressives, called "Rubénistes," argued for more color and movement. The argument was a great deal more than a discussion among second-rate theorists, or acknowledgement that the Medici cycle of Rubens was finally having a stylistic effect on French painting. Involved was a fundamental moral question of the 18th century: who is art for?

Medieval art preceded from the assumption that what is most holy, most beautiful, should be made available to everyone in a way that can be easily understood. In effect, the cathedrals of Europe constitute one of the highest levels of "mass art" ever achieved. The Renaissance forwarded a different point of view. The comprehensive ideal of Institutionalized Individualism was generated as a cultural system, which integrated the psychologically consonant developments of religious protestantism, economic capitalism, political democracy and aesthetic single-point perspective. Simultaneously arose an elitist attitude towards art, which Poussin and the Academy had incorporated. As Anthony Blunt has pointed out, when the "Rubénsistes" insisted on color *because* it could appeal to the uneducated as drawing could not, they were advocating "an almost democratic conception of art," one "challenging the view generally accepted since the early Renaissance that painting is an art appealing to the mind and only to be enjoyed by intellectuals."

So long as only a well-educated elite of two or three thousand people were the principal patrons of art, as was true for most of the 17th century, there was little argument. But as the middle class with less education and different interests, continued to grow at a geometric rate, the audience for art widened and changed shape.

One painter of genius, Chardin [Plates 10 and 11], already had started to paint for this new art patron rather than the court. As the Academy began to hold regular exhibitions, or *Salons*, for the public—annually after 1737 and biannually after 1746—the new public started to form its own aesthetic feelings and to make those feelings heard. They found their spokesman in Diderot, who began to write art criticism in 1759. In passionate reaction to the whole of the Rococo style, he judged its leader, Boucher, to be frivolous and unworthy of attention; and expressed a preference for Teniers over Watteau. To the standard vocabulary of formalist aesthetics he added the revolutionary dimension of moral and social judgment while considering the content of a work of art. For him the function of art was to make "virtue adorable and vice repugnant."

Diderot, and like-minded leaders of the "Enlightenment," looked on the discovery of the upper middle-class village of Pompeii in 1748 as something of a revelation. Rome had always meant massive temples and forums. Now it became clear that the average modern citizen could live like their Roman ancestors. All they needed to do was follow what seemed to be a "natural law" of architecture and decoration that J. J. Winckelmann in his best-selling *History of Ancient Art* was describing to them as "noble simplicity and quiet grandeur." From this predisposition arose the style of Neo-Classicism, which was assimilated by the unusually sympathetic court of Louis XVI (1774-1792) and the whole of affluent Europe for two generations.

The new attitude toward art brought the moralizing allegories of Greuze (ca. 1725-1805) to sudden fame in the 1750s, after which a school of socially oriented painting grew up around artists like Jeaurat, Lépicié, Aubrey and Boilly. A more specifically Neo-Classical style starts to emerge in the 1760s with Vien (1716-1809). Finally, in the 1780s, Diderot and Neo-Classicism found the formative genius they were looking for in the person of Jacques-Louis David (1748-1825)—an early follower of his cousin Boucher, and a pupil of Vien. At first symbolically and then administratively, David was able to lead French art to and through the Revolution of 1789.

He was a member of the revolutionary Convention which voted for the death of his former patron, Louis XVI (and the old Royal Academy) in 1793. He adroitly survived Robespierre and the "Reign of Terror" to become the principal painter of Napoleon (1769-1821), who, on the strength of his brilliant military and political leadership became the First Consul of the Republic in 1799, and was coronated Emperor by the Pope in 1804. Until his defeat at Waterloo in 1815, Napoleon ruled an extraordinary Empire. During this period, David was not only the supreme painter of France, but also the artistic director of the Emperor's successful aesthetic campaign to make most of France (and much of the Western World) believe they could become citizens of a New Rome, by sur-

rounding themselves with appropriate architecture and decoration, painting and sculpture, dress and speech.

The patrons of David, his new academy of painters, and the best sculptors of the age—Houdon (1741-1828) and Canova (1757-1822)—were those leading citizens of the upper middle class who had conducted and won the French Revolution of 1789, as they had the American Revolution of 1776, and the British Revolution of 1688. We tend to forget that it was only the well-to-do who actually won political power in all of those revolutions. In France, only 100,000 out of 6,000,000 men gained the right to vote. But the replacement of monarchy by plutocracy was the first significant step towards the ideal of complete democracy. It gave the feeling of freedom to all of the French people, who were willing in exchange to give up a million lives, a throne, and the divinity that had resided in the Cathedral of Notre Dame, which was rededicated to the Goddess of Reason.

The era to which we ourselves belong has not yet acquired a name of its own. Perhaps this does not strike us as peculiar at first—we are, after all, still in midstream— but considering how promptly the Renaissance coined a name for itself, we may well ponder the fact that no key concept comparable to the "rebirth of antiquity" has emerged in the two hundred years since our era began. It is tempting to make "revolution" such a concept, because rapid and violent change has indeed characterized the modern world. . . . The modern era began with revolutions of two kinds: the industrial revolution, symbolized by the invention of the steam engine, and the political revolution, under the banner of democracy, in America and France. Both revolutions are still going on; industrialization and democracy, as goals, are sought all over the world . . . with effects more far-reaching than any since the Neolithic Revolution ten thousand years ago. Both are founded on the idea of progress, and command an emotional allegiance that once was reserved for religion; but whereas progress in science during the past two centuries has been continuous . . . , we can hardly make this claim for man's pursuit of happiness, however we chose to define it.

Here, then, is the conflict fundamental to our era. Man today, having cast off the framework of traditional authority which confined and sustained him before, can act with a latitude both frightening and exhilarating. In a world where all values may be questioned, man searches constantly for his own identity, and for the meaning of human existence, individual and collective. . . . Modern civilization thus lacks the cohesiveness of the past; it no longer proceeds by readily identifiable periods. . . . Instead we find a continuity of another kind, that of movements and countermovements. Spreading like waves, these "isms" . . . never dominant anywhere for long . . . compete or merge with each other in endlessly shifting patterns.

H. W. JANSON

Part Two:

The Beginning of Modern Times

CONTINUING REVOLUTIONS:

1830, 1848 and 1871

The Revolution of 1789 was only the first of a series in France. Throughout the rest of the century, the development of artistic styles would be intimately connected with changes in the structure of government and society. When a Europe exhausted by war met for the peace treaties of Vienna in 1815, conservative forces of the upper middle class, respectful of tradition and fearful of anarchy, were placed in power. In France this meant the restoration of Louis XVIII (1814-1824). A limited monarchy successfully mediated between the decreasingly powerful nobility and the increasingly powerful bourgeoisie whose strength would grow throughout the century in direct proportion to the extraordinary technical and economic development of the Industrial Revolution.

This delicate political balance was not maintained under the succeeding monarchy of his brother Charles X (1824-1830), the last of the Bourbon line, who (after conquering Algeria) was anachronistic enough to try to restore "Divine Monarchy" in a country that had grown fond of its liberties. When the King dissolved the popularly elected Chamber of Deputies in July of 1830, the workers and students rioted. This unmistakable pressure resulted in the abdication of Charles X, and the succession of the "liberal" Duke of Orléans— Louis Philippe (1830-1848), "the Citizen King," who dressed and thought like a sober businessman. The success of his reign reflects the respect in which he was held by the upper middle class.

However, more liberal elements were restless under the fact that still only 200,000 of France's 8,000,000 were permitted to vote, and the fact that the sympathies of a monarchy with the needs of the middle and lower classes were not great. During the late 1840s Europe was hit with a series of economic disasters, from crop failure to the end of the railroad building boom. Widespread unemployment in France kindled discontent over frequent acts of political intolerance and shockingly infrequent responses to the social misery generated by the Industrial Revolution. In February 1848 the students and workers took to the barricades again. At the sound of the first shots Louis Philippe resigned. This time the people would settle for nothing less than a republic with universal suffrage.

The April election for the National Assembly of the Second Republic was the first of European history in which the entire adult male population of a country was allowed to vote. And yet, owing to a curious trait in the French national character, the man these new democrats elected to be their president was Louis Napoleon Bonaparte, nephew of the former Emperor. With broad popular support, he was able to declare himself the head of a Second Empire in 1852. Under this more or less benevolent dictatorship, business prospered and the arts flourished, until the crush of Bismarck's

army in the Franco-Prussian War of 1870-1871. After that humiliating defeat, France would no longer toy with old ideas of monarchistic grandeur. By now the economic power of the middle class was strong enough to defeat the socialist uprising of 1871 (known as the *Commune*), and to take effective political control of the country, a control it continues to retain.

After Napoleon's defeat at Waterloo in 1815, France as a military force would never again hold a position of European dominance. And France was no longer looked upon as the only country which produced all of the most brilliant painters and sculptors. By now almost every part of Western Europe and America was producing geniuses of its own. French artists became increasingly open to inspiration from artists in other countries, such as Goya, Constable, Turner, and the Pre-Raphaelites. Nevertheless, throughout the century, France remained the cultural capital of the West—the country in which most of the more important movements developed most fruitfully. There would be many more of these movements or "isms" than ever before, lasting much shorter periods of time. Western culture, being woven ever closer together by rapidly improving communications, started to take on the complexity of modern times.

NEW PATRONS OF ART:

Discomfort and Despair

One of the primary reasons there were, and continue to be, so many "isms" is due to a radical change in the relationship between artists and patrons. The Church and the State were no longer the principal patrons. The Revolution set artists free from being the servants of this limited clientele. Most of them were the social and economic equals of their new patrons—that amorphous and extremely diverse body of individuals known collectively as the middle class. The average artist was now in a position to create anything he wanted, if someone wanted to buy it. And the average patron was free to commission anything he wanted, if he could find someone to do it. According to Arnold Hauser:

"The emergence of the middle class, with its individualism and its passion for originality, put an end to the idea of style as something consciously and deliberately held in common by a cultural community, and gave the idea of intellectual property its current significance. . . . Art ceases to become a social activity guided by objective and conventional criteria, and becomes an activity of self-expression creating its own standards; it becomes, in a word, the medium through which the single individual speaks to single individuals."

This situation sometimes encouraged the creation of important works of art. But far more often the new style of patronage, with all its plurality of tastes, produced a great deal of variety and an enormous amount of mediocrity.

The relationships between the "modern" patrons and the "modern" artists were uncomfortable at best. It soon became clear that the two parties seldom believed in the same thing. As the new order settled into its position of social dominance, it began to polarize. The better intentioned, "liberal" minority attempted to make the humanitarian ideas of the Enlightenment the practical objectives of their personal ambitions and institutional programs. But the more numerous, less sensitive majority were not so concerned with the larger social and aesthetic values. They tended to focus more narrowly on the personal economic value of industrialized materialism. Having lost faith in the broader moral values of Christianity, and swept along by the tide of spectacular industrial progress, most of these early capitalists looked on the "natural law" writings of Adam Smith as sacred scripture, and ran their business accordingly.

The new order was ill at ease in what it was being asked to do. They and their ancestors had no experience in being "patrons of the arts." Until the 1780s, the only regular supporters of artists were aristocrats. Now, as a class, history was forcing them to provide the financial support for projects they were ill equipped to understand, and therefore could not appreciate. Kenneth Clark has summarized the situation:

"On one side of the chasm was the new middle class nourished by the Industrial Revolution. . . . Sandwiched between a corrupt aristocracy and a brutalized poor, it had produced a defensive morality, conventional, complacent, hypocritical. . . . On the other side of the chasm were the finer spirits—poets, painters, novelists, who were still heirs of the Romantic movement. . . . They felt themselves —and not without reason—to be entirely cut off from the prosperous majority. They mocked at the respectable middle class and its bourgeois king, Louis Philippe, called them philistines and barbarians. But what could they put in place of the middle-class morality? They themselves were still in search of a soul."

Ways of making economic progress somehow go hand-in-hand with spiritual progress continued to elude both sides. The phenomenon of the "bohemian" began, as a race apart from the mainstream into which they were born, searching in quiet desperation for a viable alternative to what was going on all around them.

Every other dominant culture in the history of European civilization had managed, without difficulty, to find artists of genius to immortalize what they believed in most. It is a startling fact that for a hundred years this middle-class culture could not. No Le Nain or Chardin came forward to paint the factories, the railroads, or the banks; or even the moral imperative of the "White Man's Burden"—that spirit of unprecedented power and scope which brought most of the planet under the economic and political control or "influence," of Europe and America when there were no longer enough raw materials and markets at home to feed the fires of the Industrial Revolution.

Those French artists to whom the 20th century has devoted its books and exhibitions are the ones who protested against the entire civilization of In-dustrialized Technocracy. With the painters and sculptors, most of the major European poets and novelists of the century stood in conscious revolt against the dehumanization of life that was resulting from rampant materialism; and against the cultural artifacts that symbolized the bourgeois attitude of life—those shallow vessels only deep enough to contain such spiritual values as might be left over at the end of a day, when the serious business of living was over.

MIDDLE-CLASS AESTHETICS:
Facades of Feeling

To understand the artistic revolutions of the 19th century, one must understand what they were against. What were the artifacts to which progressive artists were so unalterably opposed? What was produced by and for a society which believed that art was not really "an honest day's work"? The most obvious artifacts were architectural. As E. H. Gombrich has noted, "the amount of building done in the nineteenth century was probably greater than in all the former periods taken together." The architectural environments with which individuals or societies chose to surround themselves are, perhaps, the most expressive self-portraits of the inarticulate. The buildings commissioned by the bourgeoisie speak loudly and clearly.

With the ease of selecting a wallpaper pattern, they built their homes, office buildings and civic monuments in every style that could be found in the catalogue of history: Neo-Classic, Neo-Gothic, Neo-Baroque, Neo-Rococo and Neo-Byzantine, et cetera, punctuated by a plethora of miscellaneous mixtures. This kind of patronage may be characterized as Historicism. It resulted in work that was often distinctive, and sometimes charming, but basically little more than redundant renderings of styles developed in previous centuries by other cultures. It was mostly facades, as false as their attitudes toward their fellow human beings.

Characteristic of the century's aesthetic schizophrenia was the fact that in 1806 Napoleon, on the advice of David, established a separate *École des Beaux-Arts*, insuring that architects would be educated in one school, and engineers another. As a result, the architects were prepared to serve up almost any historical stone salad that a city's building committee could agree upon. None of them were aware that the most significant building material of the century was cast iron.

Although the middle class refused to admit it (because they were told that what they were seeing was not "art") the greatest architectural achievements of the century were created by engineers who believed in what they were doing, and proceeded on concrete assumptions which were firmly rooted in reality. In the bridges, and the exhibition monuments, such as the Crystal Palace of 1851 and the Eiffel Tower of 1889, can be seen the aesthetic flowering of the Industrial Revolution. Here are lines as straight as the linearity of pragmatic thinking. Here are curves that have the form they do primarily because they conform to the economic morality of practical purpose. Here is the philosophy and theology of the century made manifest.

No entirely original architectural style would be generated until the Art Nouveau (or "new art") at the end of the century, when the most important architects began to utilize the principles and materials of engineering in the quest for the articulation of modern reality.

The dominant bourgeois attitude throughout the century was equally eclectic towards painting and sculpture. Popular patronage wanted the subject matter obvious (preferably a moral allegory); the feeling as sentimental as the novels they gave

FIGURE 7: *Palais des Beaux-Arts* during Queen Victoria's Visit.
Wood engraving, *The Illustrated London News,* 1 September 1855.
Culver Pictures, Inc.

their children to read; and the style securely anchored in the justification of being like something that had been done before.

Decade after decade, the *École des Beaux-Arts* continued to turn out talented painters and sculptors who could fulfill these wishes. During the Bourbon restoration of Louis XVIII and Charles X (1814-1830) most patrons found the edges of David's art too hard. Influenced by the singular genius of the independent Ingres (1780-1867), the second ranking artists of the day—such as Prud'hon (1758-1823), Girodet (1767-1824), Gérard (1770-1837) and Guérin (1774-1833)—accommodated

FIGURE 8: Jean Léon Gérôme, *The Bath*, ca. 1880-1885.
Oil on canvas,
The Fine Arts Museums of San Francisco.
Mildred Anna Williams Fund, 1961

their less cerebral audience by softening the sharp edges of classical subject matter with the warmth of sentiment. The formula of sensuous figure-forms being placed in exotic settings—whether ancient, Arabian, or simply rustic—continued to typify the style and subject matter that the taste-setting *Salon* (sometimes frequented by 10,000 paying visitors a day) would prefer to the end of the century. During the later 1800s, the best loved practitioners of this craft were Couture (1815-1879), Cabanel (1823-1889), Gérôme (1824-1904) and Bouguereau (1825-1905). Their polished nudes are very like their earlier sisters, except that in response to a number of artistic developments, including the advent of photography, they became more realistic. This is the kind of art which all the artists represented in this exhibition were against.

ROMANTIC CLASSICISM:

Classicism and/or Romanticism

Students of art history are usually taught that there were two very different styles that dominated the earlier 19th century. First was "Neo-Classicism," which matured in the 1780s, and continued to act as the principal influence on most important painters and sculptors until about 1820. The first leader of the movement was David; and the second, David's only pupil of equal genius, Ingres. Then, in the late teens and early 1820s, the imagination of younger artists was captured by the powerful stylistic innovations of Géricault and Delacroix. This new movement, called "Romanticism," continued as the principal influence until about 1850, when a new generation of "Realists" exerted their presence publically.

As with most simplifications, from art history or any other intellectual discipline, there is some truth in looking at events this way. Diametrically opposed artistic qualities can be seen in comparing much of the work of David with much of the work of Delacroix [Plate 16]. These qualities appealed to very different attitudes among the new patrons of art.

In the earlier part of the century, more patrons enjoyed an art that was based on the study of ancient statues and the quiet perfection of Raphael. They responded to clearly presented subject-matter that was firmly delineated, with only a "reasonable" amount of smooth, cool color applied between the lines with almost invisible brushstrokes. They liked compositions which were obviously balanced into equilibrium, and as compactly focused as a statically symmetrical stage-set. Part of the reason this style was so influential is because David had decided to paint this way. And part of the reason is because its aesthetic qualities of the style gave his audience something they wanted to have, this audience that was looking for a disciplined way to confront the chaos of a new world order.

In the second quarter of the century, more patrons were confident enough in themselves and their now secure position in the world, that they were able to respond to a more dynamic idea of art and life. Inspired by the power of the Manneristic Michelangelo and the Baroque force of Rubens, Géricault and Delacroix reopened their asymmetrical compositions toward infinity. Instead of the cool, clear, even light of reason, they probed into the tensely contrasting dark and light of uncertainty and mystery. They poured heat into their colors, and let energy and passion manifest itself through the undulation of every line.

Historically, it is important to remember that the "classicizing" trend is not something that began one way, continued in one direction only, and then suddenly ended. Nor is the "romanticizing" trend something that began when "classicizing" ended. Both stylistic traits have similar points of departure, and continually cross-fertilize each other. These two polarities existed as aspects of each other from their first stirrings in the earlier 18th century, through their mutual maturing be-

tween the 1780s and the 1820s. The idea of becoming like a Roman was just as "romantic" as wanting to become an Arab, or a knight in King Arthur's court. And, for all their differences, it was just as "classicizing" for Delacroix to choose the Baroque model of Rubens for his guide, as it was for David to select the Baroque model of Poussin. The ostensibly opposing attitudes can be found side by side, not only in the collections of single patrons, but also in the work of single artists. David and Gros could, at times, be as colorful and emotional as Delacroix. Delacroix, at times, could be as restrained as they. Formally, the two threads of Romanticism and Classicism weave around each other like a double helix.

FIGURE 9: Detail from Eugéne Delacroix, Plate 16.

Psychologically, both positions within Romantic Classicism express dissatisfaction with the here and now, and a yearning for something more meaningful. Sociologically, both styles are the result of a society in the midst of spiritual turmoil, searching for a new way to live. Artists were offering two different alternatives. Perhaps the most important difference is that David and the conservative members of the middle class, believing in the guides of tradition and reason, responded to that stylistic polarity within Romantic Classicism that reassured them by articulating the same belief. Those responding to the "romantic" polarity received aesthetic reinforcement of their belief that intuition and feeling were more important guides to experience. The "classic" artist and patron were evolutionary, tending to believe that society and art could only be restored to former greatness by the collective effort of everyone, with a limited amount of freedom, moving forward slowly. The "romantic" artist and patron were revolutionary, tending to believe that society can improve significantly only when each individual explores his own sensibility with absolute freedom.

During the first quarter of the 19th century even the most important artists continued to share in the eclectic, historicizing attitude of the new middle class, of which they too were a part (whether they liked it or not). They were looking backward in time for stylistic points of departure and subject matter, and in doing so they were continuing a tradition honored since the Renaissance. David was looking back through Poussin to ancient Rome. Prud'hon was trying to become a modern Correggio. Michel was looking at landscape again with the eyes of Rembrandt. Ingres [Plate 15]— the most profound draftsman of the century—was inspired to create an extraordinary synthesis of the formal principles which underlay the art of both Raphael and the Mannerists. He carried the primacy of line to such an ultimate extreme that it becomes reminiscent of the School of Fontainebleau. And Delacroix succeeded in becoming what he desired to be—the spiritual grandson of Rubens

and the great grandson of Michelangelo.

During the second quarter of the century, however, there is a subtle but extremely significant shift in the artist's approach to time. The Renaissance idea was that a painter should reconstruct an illusion of the past, in a dramatic, quasi-theatrical setting. By making time stand still in such an abstraction, the assumption was that the artist's audience was being presented with a lasting symbol of all time.

The grandeur implicit in this approach continues to be an influence throughout the era of Romantic Classicism. All these artists were attracted by the idea of looking at vast panoramas of interior or exterior space. But the primary reference gradually shifts, from the abstract time of history, to the real time of the present. The greatest masterpieces of these decades represent actual events. Constable's *Hay Wain* of 1821 and Turner's spectacular stormy seas of the 1820s and 1840s are the results of direct experience. Turner even went so far as to have himself strapped to the mast of a ship in a storm. In France, the most important works are also of contemporary subject-matter: Géricault's *Raft of the Medusa* in 1819; Delacroix's *The Massacre at Chios* in 1824, and *Liberty Leading the People* in 1830.

Delacroix was so impressed by Constable's *Hay Wain* (a gold medal winner at the Paris *Salon* of 1824) that he took his *The Massacre at Chios* down from the walls of that exhibition in order to increase the naturalism of his landscape. The classical, narrative tradition of Poussin and Claude was losing its persuasiveness. The little allegorical figures at the bottom of landscape paintings started to disappear. Artists were looking at the landscape around them for its own sake, with fresh eyes.

What was moving art from a fixation on the past towards a devotion to the present? Two of the major forces were moral and philosophical. Social consciousness—an intense awareness of the effect of contemporary political events on the quality of human life—manifested itself throughout Romantic Classicism to a degree that has not been seen in the history of art before or since. This awareness produced an unusual number of masterpieces between David's *Marat* of 1793 and Goya's *The Third of May, 1808;* to Delacroix's immortalization of the Revolution of 1830; Daumier's of the Revolution of 1848; and Manet's *Execution of Maximilian* in 1867. This trend helped to move artistic thinking towards the face of current realities. But interest in such subject-matter soon disappeared, and would not be seen again until the World Wars of the 20th century. Realizing that the outward act of doing a political painting was not the most effective tool for changing social conditions, most of the progressive artists turned their attention inwardly, in search of what could be accomplished by conducting a spiritual revolution inside themselves.

The long-range influence underlying the development of naturalism or realism in the arts was the operative assumption—fundamental to almost all modern philosophy since the Enlightenment—that truth is best revealed by focusing full attention on the facts before one's eyes. The painters of traditional Christian theology from the Middle Ages to William Blake, did not accept this belief in the primacy of material reality. But the attitude of Scientific Empiricism or Logical Positivism—so clearly articulated by Hume and Comte, and represented by Marx and Darwin—became the basic assumption of the modern world during the 19th century. As the high purposes and objective values of the physical sciences entered that public pantheon of the unquestionably true, scientific materialism and economic determinism joined together as the philosophy of modern man.

NATURALISM:

Phase One: Barbizon

This new belief in the primary value of direct experience, and in the possibility of perceiving the most valued realities within the physical world, also led a group of painters to start another artistic revolution. This revolution began when a few young men left their dark studios in order to paint nature in the open air, and did not end until Impressionism was over. This new love of the natural, this new rejection of "any interest unborrowed from the eye" was responsible for what John Ruskin and Kenneth Clark have called "the nineteenth century's great contribution to the history of art"—the flowering of landscape painting.

The "nature" these young painters were looking at was one the Western World had never seen before. Before the writings of Jean-Jacques Rousseau in the middle of the 18th century, the word "nature" had a meaning not much larger than the phrase "common sense" does today. Throughout the Middle Ages; during the eras of Renaissance, Baroque and Rococo art; no one derived any deep pleasure from looking at the natural landscape. During the Age of Enlightenment, naturalistic detail and vivid emotions were sublimated into formalized ideals. While most philosophers were formulating eternal, predictable laws for the physical universe, social commentators recommended similar restraint. Nature was most enjoyed when best controlled, as in the English garden. As for raw nature, it was sufficiently repulsive that cultivated individuals drew the blinds as their coaches passed through the unedited scenery of the Alps.

Then, suddenly Rousseau looked at the Alps and saw (in the words of Thomas Grey) that "not a precipice, not a torrent, not a cliff, but is pregnant with religion and poetry." As Arnold Hauser has said: "the depth and extent of Rousseau's influence are without precedent. He is one of those minds which, like Marx and Freud in more recent times, changed the thinking of millions within a single generation." Rousseau expanded the idea of nature so that it embraced the full scope of Divinity. It was a welcome relief from the dry agnosticism of Voltaire and the Encyclopedists. For those who were not persuaded by Christianity, Science, or Economic Materialism, Rousseau's Nature offered a new way by which a person could establish a metaphysically satisfying relationship with the universe. The great poets of the early 19th century —such as Wordsworth, Coleridge, Byron, and Keats—served the new Goddess of Nature with words of such beauty that a new, and even larger generation of millions were converted by their profound Pantheism.

The Barbizon painters were among these converts. John Canaday's presentation of the philosophy of their leader, Théodore Rousseau (1812-1867), is representative of the thinking that went into this revolutionary approach to landscape painting:

"He is so impressed with nature as a force that every irregularity in the growth of a tree, every blade of green . . . every cloud . . . , has for him its own vigorous life as part of a purposeful scheme . . . , to conceal or change any part of the natural miracle would be only to weaken it. He sees no need to put it into a classical order because he feels a more powerful order behind the growth of things, the turn of the seasons, the rising or setting of the sun. He painted images of this cycle of omnipotent force as men have always painted images of their gods, but he did not have to fabricate an image because it was everywhere for him to see."

To confront nature directly, and through that immediate reality establish a meaningful, individual relationship with the universe—that was the objective of this first generation of naturalists, as it would be for the second generation who would become known as Impressionists. Gradually, the strength of this desire to intimately interrelate with nature outgrew the boundaries of religion in the formally organized sense. It simply became the daily purpose of being alive. Consciously or un-

consciously, the direction and the intensity of the desire remained the same. Until the end of his life, Monet wanted to "fuse with nature" as passionately as Wordsworth. Pissarro was speaking for all of the Impressionists when he wrote: "salvation lies in nature."

Landscape was not a well appreciated subject in the official circles of the *Salon* at the beginning of the century. The official *Prix de Rome* that was established for this category in 1817 was only for "historical landscape." Most of the few who practiced landscape painting continued to look at the outside world as Poussin had. What they actually saw was intellectualized into a carefully balanced pattern of horizontals and verticals which receded in depth by a clear succession of logical steps. The abstract idea of a tree or a leaf, rather than its actual tonal appearance, was delineated with hard, dark outlines.

Painting landscape out-of-doors was not entirely unknown in the first decades of the 19th century. Corot's teachers recorded their preliminary observations in the open air, and even exhibited their work in the *Salons*, but only as "sketches." The finished compositions were always "completed" in the studio. By the early 1820s an increasing number of painters started to gather regularly during the summers in the forest of Fontainebleau, especially around the village of Barbizon, about thirty miles from Paris. The greatest genius of them all—Corot (1796-1875) [Plates 19 and 20] gravitated there in 1822; the brilliant young Rousseau arrived in 1827 at the age of 15. During the 1830s a group of important painters began to work together informally as friends with common interests. Remembered as the Barbizon School, under the spiritual leadership of Rousseau and Corot, its principal "members" included Diaz (1807-1876), Troyon (1810-1865), Dupré (1811-1889), Jacques (1813-1894), Millet (1814-1875) and Daubigny (1817-1878) [Plate 21].

The July Revolution of 1830 was extremely important to their life and work. Almost all of them were ardent radicals who detested Charles X. Their sympathies were with the liberal Orleanist party, from which came most of their first patrons including the Citizen-King himself. During the two decades of his reign, the Barbizon painters developed their mature styles, and successfully conducted an uphill battle with the Academy. Their inspiration came from many sources, not only the British examples of Constable, Bonington and others, but also 17th century prototypes from the Flemish and Dutch.

As the upper middle class continued to exercise its new authority, it showed itself to be guilty of the same kind of inhumanity that the aristocratic power structure did. One by one, the disillusioned painters, these "men of 1830," left the city for the spiritually superior quality of life they felt they could find in the country. (Most of the Impressionists and Post-Impressionists would follow them.) There they continued the century-long revolt against industrialization. Of the kindred spirits in their generation, only Daumier [Plates 17 and 18] stayed behind in the city, where he chronicled the reasons why some of the most sensitive people were leaving the city, and still are. Their feeling for the good of the country ran as deep as their love of nature. Millet, Rousseau, Dupré and Jacques all fought on the barricades during the Revolution of 1848.

During the short-lived Republican victory of four years, the first phase of 19th century Romanticism was superseded by the new Naturalism or Realism in both landscape and figure painting. The radical principle of a non-juried *Salon* was established for 1848 and 1849. Daumier was confident enough to exhibit his paintings for the first time. Corot finally displayed an out-of-doors study, and open-air painting of a French site. The new director of fine arts, Charles Blanc, believed in an art of actuality, which could be comprehended (at least in part) by anyone. State commissions were awarded to Millet, Rousseau, Daubigny and Dupré. The Le Nains and Chardin were "rediscovered."

With the advent of the Second Empire (1852-

1870) the revolutionary spirit of Naturalism was quickly submerged. In the public arena, the light of trees and the people of the soil were overshadowed by polite portraits, theatrical battle scenes and innumerable allegories of Venus. During this era, the artists whom Imperial taste made famous were Gérôme, Cabanel, Bouguereau, Meissonier, Winterhalter and Rosa Bonheur.

FIGURE 10: Detail from Charles Daubigny, Plate 21.

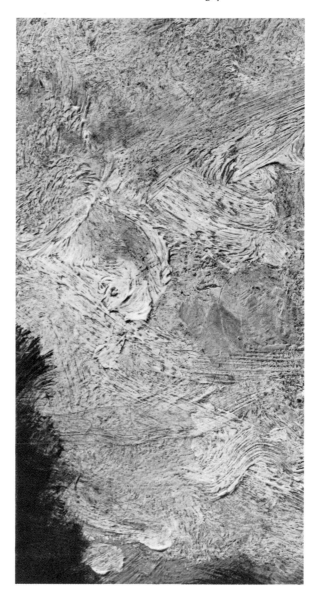

However, Napoleon III was too clever a politician to disregard the Barbizon School completely; and their clientele was already sturdy enough to guarantee these painters a certain amount of financial security, even without a great deal of royal patronage. Throughout the 1850s and 1860s the most progressive painters continued to be the first generation of Naturalists, and the next generation of Naturalists which the Barbizon artists were inspiring towards Impressionism.

The most important contributions of the former to the latter were the tradition of painting out-of-doors in natural light, and the idea of trying to capture direct impressions of nature in her transitory aspects. As a result of the process of trying to capture those impressions in natural light, a fundamental change developed in both their technique and the physical appearance of the canvas [Plate 21]. Robert Herbert has analyzed this development succinctly:

". . . In the 1830s, the Barbizon artists were still much aware of the architecture of trees and their autonomous existence in illusionary space, but shortly after the mid-century, memory knowledge of touchable, solid masses yielded to the optical, so purged of non-visual experience that the dabs of pigment began to float free of imaginary substance. When that occurred, the artist became as much interested in the dabs as in what they represented, and by the early sixties they were all painting in a variety of small strokes whose colors, no longer blended one with another, took on new life. Earth colors, the customary matrix for brighter hues, began to wane when that matrix was no longer used, and a lighter palette was the result. Concentration on the purely visual appearance of things also produced a tendency toward greater flatness which was abetted by the choice of a narrower focal range. The Barbizon painters began to restrict their slice of nature to what the eye can see without moving back and forth, in place of the traditional panorama."

NATURALISM:
Phase Two: Realist

Realism in figure painting is usually dated from the unjuried *Salons* of 1848 and 1849, when Millet exhibited *The Sower*, and Courbet received a medal for his *Burial at Ornans*. After 1848, Courbet [Plates 22-26] was the most conspicuous leader of the revolution against the Academy. He regularly enjoyed a *"succès du scandale"* at each of the *Salons* after 1849. In 1853 the Emperor threatened to attack one of his canvases with a whip. His position as *chef d'école* was firmly established at the *Exposition Universelle* of 1855, where he had the audacity to set up an exhibition of his work that the jury had rejected, accompanied by a manifesto of "Realism." For two decades he probably was the most talked about artist in Paris. "Show me an angel and I will paint one," he said. With the heavy brown axe of his art he chopped away at the frivolous anecdotes of eclecticism. The extraordinary strength of his personality, as a painter and as a person, was a primary influence on the collective decision of the next generation to concentrate exclusively on the subject matter of contemporary life. He succeeded in establishing the truth of what all novelists already knew, that everyday life contains at least as much nobility and poetry as any subject from history or myth.

There were many aspects of his art for which the generation of Impressionism would no longer have any use—the darkness of his color; his traditional need to create proselytizing, *Salon*-size images of gigantic scale; and that self-conscious semi-realism by which he painted allegorical compositions that looked like they took place but actually did not. The Impressionists would proceed past the wider time reference of Courbet and the Barbizon painters into a devotion to only the moment in which they were living. But the example of Courbet would be of considerable assistance in helping them find a way to get inside that moment.

FIGURE 11: Detail from Édouard Manet, Plate 29.

The sincerity of his less fabricated approach to landscape, both at its most complex [Plates 23 and 24] and its most simple [Plate 22] is as deep as any in the distinguished history of French landscape. His images of "real life" have a presence that is so highly tactile it is almost tangible. These images are often rendered freely and thickly with a palette knife, and anticipate the sensuous dimensionality of Impressionist technique.

Courbet's historical position, summarizing as it does much of what had taken place within the Naturalistic movement and anticipating what would follow, is so important that it may be thought of as the fulcrum of French art at mid-century. His style would influence not only Manet, Degas, Monet, Renoir, Fantin [Plate 27] and Bazille [Plate 38], but also Cézanne and Gauguin.

If Courbet may be seen as a fulcrum, it was Édouard Manet (1832-1882) [Plate 28 and 29] who actually tipped the scale of history in the direction that painting would continue to follow for the next hundred years. The artistic revolution he conducted single-handedly was the first of the most fundamental in the century. Like all the artists who, with Courbet, were pursuing a realistic style in the 1850s and 1860s, Manet was deeply influenced by the 17th century Spanish paintings in the Orléans Collection, which was made public after the fall of Louis Philippe in 1848. His single, standing figures of the 1860s [Plate 29] show how strongly Manet felt the Baroque realism of Velázquez and Zurbarán.

But Manet was inspired by these Spanish masters to do with Realism something of which Courbet never dreamed. Courbet's approach to painting figures or objects was basically the same that had been employed since the Renaissance. The picture frame was thought of as a window on the visible world. There one saw represented what could actually be seen. This illusion was created in a pictorial space that was defined by the 15th century principles of single vanishing-point perspective.

This convention dictates that objects should be placed inside an artificial space that has a foreground, a middle distance and a background. In the background, the imaginary straight lines which begin at the four corners of the canvas, and act like walls holding in the space, all meet and disappear at a single vanishing-point. In order to give the illusion of three-dimensional roundness, objects within the pictorial space are gradually modeled in half-tones between lightness and darkness, usually from a single source of illumination.

This is still the way most paintings are done today, by amateur and professional alike. But Manet was the first to question this five-hundred-year-old assumption, and provide a very different but equally valid alternative. He approached the idea of time and space in art from a radically new point of departure.

Space in the panoramic vistas of Naturalism, through the Barbizon School to Courbet, is of great breadth and filled with considerable detail. Those complex allegories of reality require that one takes a long period of time to see everything in the painting. Manet, in John Canaday's words, wanted "to capture the immediacy of instant vision." He wanted to paint in a way that would capture the first impression one has when looking at reality. To achieve a representation of what is perceived in this very short period of time, he used a simple but revolutionary set of assumptions.

Manet's first assumption was philosophical. He, like all the Impressionists, was distrustful of intellectual generalizations. Although he left us few words of his own, we may learn something of his thinking from the expressed ideas of his close friend, Stéphane Mallarmé (1842-1898) whom Manet saw almost every day for ten years. Anne Coffin Hanson has summarized their mutual desires as follows: "Mallarmé strove to eliminate unnecessary words from his poetry and to depend on the evocative effect of precisely chosen images. In a letter of 1864 he announces his aim: 'To paint not the thing, but the effect which it produces.'"

The word that Mallarmé most specifically wanted to eliminate from the vocabulary of poetry was the word "like" (comme). In the interest of communicating the effect or impression of a thing directly and quickly, Mallarmé wanted to remove the time-consuming tradition of simile or metaphor which allude to reality only indirectly. That Manet's ambitions were similar is clear from his own words: "Concision in art is a necessity. . . . The verbose painter bores; who will get rid of all these trimmings?" By working within a momentary idea of time, Manet was rejecting the entire tradition of elaborated simile, metaphor and allegory upon which Academic art was based [Plate 29].

He rigorously eliminates all unessential narrative allusions. He did not wish to tell a long "story" with many details. He wanted to tell a powerful "story" with one singular image, which would have one singular effect. Every piece of subject matter is there primarily for the sake of its visual presence. In the interest of conveying the immediate impression freshly, he articulated his image directly on a white canvas with vigorous brushstrokes that have a rich reality of their own. He replaced the idea of "finish" and the technique of glazing with a pigment of such luminosity that nothing else was needed.

He tightly compresses the tradition of half-tone modeling into extremely shallow outlines around the figure forms. At the same time he loosens up the binding idea of single-point perspective to a remarkable degree. He no longer draws clear dividing lines between foreground, middle ground and background. He makes the floor and the wall, as he said, "disappear" into each other. As a result, his figure-forms flatten out toward a dramatic two-dimensionality, which one critic scoffingly compared to "a playing card." Unrestricted by the anchoring linearity of mathematic perspective, his forms float forward towards the picture-plane— that basic, aesthetic component of a painting which hovers like the membrane of an energy-field on the physical, two-dimensional surface of a canvas.

All of the psychological and formal implications of space and time interacting freely would not start to be explored until the New Art which followed Impressionism in the 1880s. But Manet was the first to move painting towards the primary assumption that began with the so-called Post Impressionists, and has continued throughout the 20th century. This assumption, articulated by Maurice Denis (1870-1943) in the 1880s, is that "a picture—before being a horse, a nude, or an anecdote— is essentially a flat surface covered with colors assembled in a certain order." For having begun that abstract direction, Manet is frequently thought of as the first truly "modern" painter by the historians who date the beginnings of contemporary art from the appearance of Manet's *Luncheon on the Grass* at the *Salon des Refusés* of 1863. Actually, several more steps had to be taken before 20th century painting could begin. But Manet did take the first extraordinary step, without which the second and third steps could not have followed as they did.

NATURALISM:

Phase Three: Impressionist

In one sense, Manet already had begun the Impressionist style. He had established the basic assumptions on which the movement would continue to develop. He had "discovered" that the picture-plane is the primary arena in which to conduct the act of painting. And he worked from the new, momentary time reference, desiring to capture the instantly perceivable reality of one's first impression. During the pivotal decade of the 1860s, a younger generation of painters, inspired by Manet's direction, would build a great deal on his foundations.

"Manet's gang"—as one critic called them— was made up of those artists who are usually thought of as the core of the Impressionist group: Monet [Plate 35], Renoir [Plate 36], Pissarro [Plate 39], and Sisley [Plate 40]. The style associated with them was labeled "Impressionism" during their first joint exhibition in 1874. By deciding to exhibit as a group, independent of the *Salon*, this generation declared its open war against the Academy

—a war that took them a long, hard decade or two to win.

Led by Monet, the first important thing the younger group did with Manet's "impressionism" was to take it out of doors, back to the forests of Fontainebleau. There and in Paris, throughout the later 1860s, the group drew heavily on the previous phases of Naturalism or Realism: both the figurative innovations of Courbet and Manet, and the landscape developments of the Barbizon painters. And more.

Like every new movement in the history of art, the Impressionists were able to draw on all the painting that had preceded them, as well as all the innovations that were taking place in their contemporary world. Among the numerous resources they chose to be influenced by in their formative years were: the sensuality in the courtly art of Rococo; the light-reflecting impasto of Constable; the luminous mist in the landscapes of Venice and Turner; the vertical view-points and "floating" space of Japanese prints; the numerous insights into the nature of light and vision offered by the new technique of photography, and the color theories of scientists like Chevreul and Helmholz; as well as the energetic brush work of Delacroix, who realized that no object has only one color in it, and that pure, unmixed hues placed side by side, will "fuse naturally at a certain distance."

In the bright sunlight and open air, Monet and his friends began to paint landscapes unlike any that had ever been seen before. The Barbizon School painted landscapes of darkness. They tended to work with the deep shadows of dusk and dawn. An Impressionist might say that the Barbizon painters did not stay outside long enough. Under the influence of Romantic Classicism, most of them finished their canvases in the studio. They were after the broad view of nature's image. They took a long, meditative look at the general image that the solid reality of nature offers the eye. They were not interested in movement. Almost nothing moves inside their compositions; nor is there any abstract sense of motion in their carefully controlled technique. They were not interested in air. They were not interested in the changes of times. Their panoramas are abstract allegories of what nature looks like standing still.

Monet and his friends looked through a shorter slice of time at a smaller piece of space. They were interested in the more comprehensive and intrinsically vibrant reality that dwells inside each moment before it changes into the next. Wanting to capture all the aspects of nature's transitory existence, the young Impressionists not only began but finished their canvases out-of-doors. Before them only Daubigny and Boudin [Plate 34] were doing that regularly. And to experience nature in its ripest complexity, they chose to paint in the bright sun. Under the impact of light at its brightest, they saw that nothing is black or grey outside. Even shadows contain colors. So they eliminated from their palettes that color range which was so important for Manet; and began to use lighter and lighter hues, concentrating on the primary colors (red, yellow, blue) and their complementaries (orange, green, violet).

To capture the momentary "effect" or "impression" of a figure in a dark setting was one problem —one that Manet had solved. But how can one capture all the shimmering quality of colored light outside? Monet's genius came up with a radically new approach [Plate 35]. He would represent the object not in terms of the form he knew the object to have, but in terms of the image which the light from the object reflected into the retina of his eye. In this way, the image that he was capturing on the canvas was not the intellectualized, hard outline around a tactile object, but the purely visual, vibrating halo of colored light surrounding it. Intuitively reaching out for a way to capture the sensations of this image, he evolved a vocabulary of short, rapidly executed strokes which enabled him to represent those wavelengths of open-ended energy that he could feel moving through the air and earth and water all around him.

Working closely with his good friend Renoir, their canvases became more and more drenched with highly keyed light, and the short rapid strokes of lines, commas and dots start to fill the picture plane with a visual activity of their own [Plate 36]. By 1869, when they were working together at Argenteuil, the hundreds of strokes laid down in the actual process of painting take on a visual interest equal to that of the ostensible subject-matter.

But by then a technique had been evolved for capturing that which was their real subject matter: the energized vision of colored light, in the fullness of a single moment. To dematerialize the corporeality of any obvious reality in an aesthetically valid way is a singular achievement in itself. But also to materialize the less obvious realities of time and light and color in a way that all the levels of reality reinforce each other is the singular contribution of Monet.

Through the 1870s—the primary decade of Impressionism as a whole—all of the artists associated with the group which exhibited together worked within that single moment of experience that Manet had discovered indoors, and Monet outdoors. What each of them perceived inside this moment, and how they chose to articulate it, differ of course, just as each artist within any historical style differs significantly from one another.

Manet and Degas [Plates 30-33] preferred the figurative, urban subject matter of the upper middle class to which they belonged, along with Berthe Morisot and Mary Cassatt [Plate 42]. Monet, Pissarro [Plate 39], and Sisley [Plate 40] and the older Lépine [Plate 41] tended to prefer the countryside. Renoir was at ease in both worlds. This distinction should not be overemphasized, however. Many of them painted the landscapes of the city, as well as the landscapes outside it. And the rural landscapes they painted were often seen with the eyes of an urban visitor rather than a native. The stylistic polarities within the group ranged as far apart as Monet's transubstantiation of material to Degas, who saw no need to give up the outline quality of sculptural bulk which Ingres had taught him.

But by the end of the decade, even Degas and Manet had followed the lead of Monet and Renoir in permitting the artistically intoxicating qualities of bright, broadly stroked color to take primacy over their older insistence on recognizable facial features [Plate 33]. Degas—the most reluctant Impressionist of them all (the traditionalist who was still painting Grecian allegories when Manet painted *Olympia*) gradually reached the point where he was capturing the visual "effect" of dancers during the split second they were on their toes, and rendering the "impression" of a sparkling ring with a single dab of paint [Plate 32].

All of the Impressionists have this in common: They worked exclusively from what they could see before their eyes. Of what they could see, they wanted to capture only as much as can be perceived in a momentary glance. Each of those momentary glances—those highly selected visual sensations—is deliberately intensified by using a highly keyed palette and a series of rapidly executed strokes, which over and above the visual presence of the ostensible subject-matter, give the picture plane a rich aesthetic presence of its own.

NEW ART:
Post-Impressionism and/or Symbolism

In 1882 the French government gave Manet the Legion of Honor he had always coveted. The acceptance of Impressionism by the Academy was becoming visible at the *Salons*. By the time of the eighth and last Impressionist exhibition in 1886, most of the critics (and much of the public) considered the Impressionists serious artists, and finally began to relieve many of them of the poverty they had been enduring for two decades. The revolution of this generation had been won. Entering the popular pantheon of acceptable art styles, the Impressionist School would inspire a second generation of followers throughout every part of Europe and America.

By the early 1880s, most of the major painters who worked with the stylistic principles of Impressionism in the 1870s moved on towards a radically different kind of style, which has been vaguely labeled Post Impressionism. By this time Naturalism or Realism as a whole—including its final Impressionistic phase—had lost its power to act as a cohesive force on most of the advanced painters and sculptors of the time. It was no longer the principal force of change. A new artistic revolution was underway—one which would prove to be not only more important than Impressionism, or any other Naturalistic innovation of the 19th century, but the most important revolution in the history of Western art since the conquest of the medieval spirit by the Renaissance.

The new art which flourished between the early 1880s and the early 1900s was of profound significance in the formation of modern consciousness. This convoluted period of time served as both the deathbed for a reluctantly departing 19th century, and the cradle for the precocious arrival of our own. The 20th century was bringing with it one of the most abrupt changes in the history of the human consciousness.

Beneath the objective rationalism of Déscartes, Freud was discovering the emotional foundations of reasoned behavior. The formerly absolute and static world view of Newton was gradually dissolving into the space/time relativity of Einstein. Previously unquestioned assumptions about the very nature of life were collapsing at the corners of every traditional philosophy.

The comfortable reality assumed by the Impressionists to be commonplace was no longer so obvious or so simple. The most influential thinkers of the century—from Hegel and Marx to Darwin and Bergson—taught that what we experience as reality is not an accomplished fact but a very temporary moment of dynamic metamorphoses, an ever-continuing process with component elements interacting as completely as the pulsations of wavelengths traveling through the universe. Existence is in continuous flux. Value judgments, like "progress," depend on one's point of view, be it capitalistic, communistic or poetic. The world was forming itself anew.

If this is the way the world is, mankind would have to develop entirely new ways of relating to it. None of the methods developed since the Renaissance would work any more. Human thought would have to find unprecedented ways of giving form to itself. Art would have to find another point of departure from which to begin again the eternal problem of defining a viable position, in which one can be confident enough to start placing order around chaos.

The new point of departure was discovered in a place that few had looked before. For five centuries most artists looked only at the far side of reality—the one they could see on the outside of their eyes. In one short historical moment, during the 1880s and 1890s, the forefront of Western Art underwent a fundamental shift of focus—from the public world, to the private world inside one's self.

No one could come closer to the world outside than the Impressionists did. That style was the ultimate aesthetic realization of the 19th century's basic assumptions—naturalism, empiricism and materialism. If one's thinking proceeds from such assumptions, certainty lies in the sense experiences that come in from the outside world. But the new art which signals the arrival of a new century with a new consciousness assumes that such ideas about reality are only some of many possibilities. The reality of science is only part of what is true. These artists heard the call of other truths, so they turned the world around and looked inside of their own minds.

Among the artists who developed the new art in these two decades, the revolutionary aim was no longer an illusion that corresponded with what everyone could see, but an image consonant with nothing other than the relationship between what one sees and what one feels about what one sees. All of experience became valid subject-matter. Now the canvases started to show not only the naturalistic or abstract outlines of an idea, but also those outlines interwoven with the shape and color of one's emotional response to that idea. A coloured line no longer had to wrap around the contours of a physical object in the outside world, unless the artist wanted it to. A line could also illustrate a dream, a state of mind, or weave together a synthesis from several equally valid levels of reality.

Among the principal leaders of this artistic revolution were Cézanne [Plates 43 and 44], Van Gogh [Plates 45 and 46], Gauguin [Plate 47], Lautrec [Plate 48], Seurat, Rousseau [Plate 49] and Rodin. All of them contributed in different ways to the freeing of the creative imagination. Manet had already begun to formulate the new idea of space/time—one in which figure-ground relationships (fixed in one place for 500 years along the rigid linearity of mathematical perspective) gradually became more fluid. After Impressionism had pointed out the primacy of the picture-plane, figure-ground relationships were free to move forward and backwards, in, out and around it, in whatever arrangement corresponded to the artist's individual perception of interrelationships among thought and/or feeling, space and/or time. The elder Degas and Lautrec liberated line; Gauguin color, and the poetry of symbolism. Rousseau gave all the world confidence in the validity of every private fantasy. Van Gogh made emotion at its most intense fuse with colored paint in all of its own rich reality. No one has come closer to making inert matter come alive. Seurat showed how completely the mind could bring into order whatever emotions it encountered. And Cézanne opened art to the realization of how beautiful is the process of creation. His struggle was to realize the potential that can come from aesthetically recording the actual process of painting—the process of relating what can be seen with the experience one has while seeing. His spectacular achievement taught the 20th century what visual miracles can be made when figure and ground are free to interact in the equality of space/time; and objects free to influence the shape and color of each other—not as

they may be seen in the common world outside, but as they may be seen in the uncommon world of the painter's picture-plane.

What most of these artists contributed collectively to the transformation from old to new painting, Rodin almost single-handedly contributed to the change from old to new sculpture [Plates 51-53]. He disregarded the value of "high finish" as did the Impressionists. He replaced the idea of smooth polish with a surface in which every square inch is activated by the energy of his hands. He lifted all the traditional elements of the sculptor's vocabulary (volume, outline and detail) beyond the replication of obvious realities. He inflated contours to points of maximum tension. He projected into abstractly naturalistic masses the shape of symbolic thought. He discovered whole truths within fragments. And by sculpting complete ideas into only half of his rough stone, he made the world aware as never before, that order is what art makes out of chaos. The history of 20th century sculpture begins with Rodin, and continues (in no small part) through the sculptors he taught and/or encouraged—Maillol [Plates 54-63], Bourdelle, Despiau, Brancusi and Lipchitz.

Each of the great, turn-of-the-century artists was aware that they were participating in the creation of an art entirely unlike anything they had ever seen. As Cézanne said: "Une ère d'art nouveau se prépare." (An era of new art is preparing itself.) The foundations of contemporary art were being constructed. All the "isms" that followed in France and throughout the world during the first half of the 20th century—Fauvism, Expressionism, Cubism, Surrealism, et cetera, would be based on the new assumptions of reality that these artists in one extraordinary generation had managed to articulate. We all think and look at the world differently now, because of them. Their collective achievement was to give the 20th century a meaningful stance from which to face the problem of being alive: one foot in the world outside one's self, and one foot firmly planted in a dream.

44

Catalogue of the Exhibition

This catalogue is arranged in an approximate chronological order. The date of each work is given after the
title. If the date is given in parentheses it is because the
year does not actually appear on the work itself, but has
been determined by historical references and/or stylistic
analysis. Dimensions are given in inches and centi-
meters, height preceding width. As a rule, literary references have been limited to those which mention or
discuss the individual work being catalogued. Owing
to the complexities intrinsic to sculpture which has been
cast at different times in various editions, the Rodin
and Maillol references are both specific and general. In
the Rodin entries the years given are for the dates of the
original design. In the Maillol entries the dates are those
given by Waldemar George and/or Dina Vierny for the
first castings. References from exhibition catalogues are
cited under exhibitions.

F.L.G.

Nicolas Poussin

Born 1593 or 1594 in Normandy; died 1665.

Son of impoverished nobility, he moved to Paris about 1612. Little is known of him before 1621, when he collaborated with Philippe de Champaigne on decorations in the Luxembourg Palace (for which Rubens was painting his Marie de Médicis cycle in Antwerp during 1622-1624). In 1624 Poussin moved to Italy in order to study both classical antiquity and the art of the High Renaissance in Rome and Venice. For a short but influential time he worked in the studio of Domenichino (1581-1641), who was a leading pupil of the Carracci. By the 1630s he had freed himself from the last vestiges of the second school of Fontainebleau, developed the basic principles of his style, and started to become famous. Except for a brief visit to Paris between 1640 and 1642, when he worked for the King and Cardinal Richelieu, the rest of his life was spent in Rome. His sources of inspiration, and his clientele, were no longer at court. He was privileged to be born during that first historical moment when it was possible to enjoy an entirely different kind of patronage. Throughout Europe, growing prosperity had generated a new upper middle class of well educated, thoughtful, and leisured merchants and civil servants. It was they who supported Poussin's work. It no longer was quite so important where a painter or his patron lived. Travel was increasingly common, and communication between capitals was constant. Moreover, thanks to the formative genius of Poussin and Claude Lorrain, French art, for the first time since the middle ages, was becoming international in its appeal and influence. Although he painted very little in France, the concentrated power with which Poussin expressed his highly rational ideas was such that few artists, if any, have had a more enduring effect on the history of French painting.

1. CAMILLUS AND THE SCHOOLMASTER OF FALERII (ca. 1635-1640)
Oil on canvas, 31-7/8 x 52-3/8 in. (81 x 133 cm.)

REFERENCES
J. SMITH, *A Catalogue Raisonné of the Works of the Most Eminent Dutch, Flemish and French Painters* (1829-42), no. 175.
W. FRIEDLAENDER, "Le Maître d'Ecole Faléries châtié de sa trahison," *Gazette des Beaux-Arts,* II (1931), pp. 52 ff.
W. FRIEDLAENDER and A. BLUNT, *The Drawings of Nicolas Poussin, A Catalogue Raisonné,* II (1939), p. 12, pls. 97 & 121.
A. BLUNT, *The French Drawings in the Collection of His Majesty The King at Windsor Castle* (1945), no. 190, p. 39, pl. 37.
D. MAHON, "Poussin au carrefour des années trente," *Actes,* I (1960), p. 261.
D. MAHON, "Poussin's Early Development: An Alternative Hypothesis," *Burlington Magazine,* CII (1960), p. 303.
D. MAHON, "Poussiniana: Afterthoughts Arising from the Exhibition," *Gazette des Beaux-Arts,* CX (1962), p. 100, note 288.
A. BLUNT, *The Paintings of Nicolas Poussin, A Critical Catalogue* (1966), no. 143, pp. 102-104, repr. Fig. 143.
A. BLUNT, *Nicolas Poussin* (1967), I, p. 168, note 33, repr. II, pl. 125.

COLLECTIONS
J. Meijers (sale, Rotterdam, 9 September 1722, no. 1);
C. W. van Valkenburg (sale, Rotterdam, 11 April 1731, no. 4);
C. W. van Valkenburg (sale, Rotterdam, 7 Oct. 1733, no. 14);
The Princes of Schamburg-Lippe (by 1738);
Schamburg-Lippe (sale, Bückeburg, 3 April 1929);
Rosenbaum, Frankfort (3 April 1929);
Prince Paul of Yugoslavia (by 1934);
Böhler, Munich (1934);
Henry Levy, Strasbourg (1934);
Heirs of the Levy Estate, Paris;
Claude Lang, Brussels (by 1970);
The Norton Simon Foundation, Los Angeles (1970).

REMARKS
The subject is taken from the Roman History of Livy, Plutarch and others. When the Roman general, Furius Camillus, was besieging Falerii, a schoolmaster of that city lured some pupils to the Roman camp, offering them as hostages. Finding this act of treachery distasteful, Camillus gave the schoolmaster to his pupils for punishment.

There is a larger version of this painting in the Louvre which is traditionally dated 1637. Whether Poussin painted the smaller version shortly before or shortly after the Louvre version is not quite certain. There are preliminary drawings in the British Museum and Windsor Castle.

Claude Lorrain

Born 1600, as Claude Gellée in Lorraine; died 1682.

Of simple origins, he was orphaned at twelve, and started work as a pastry cook. As an uneducated boy of unusual sensibilities, he wandered to Italy where he became a servant and then apprentice to the Manneristic landscape painter Agostino Tassi (1581-1644). During the 1620s, he assimilated the classical landscape ideas that two other Northerners—Paul Bril (1554-1626) and Adam Elsheimer (1578-1610)—had recently developed in Italy. He also began to make studies directly from nature, as he walked through the Roman Campagna with his life-long friend and neighbor, Poussin. Like Poussin, Claude returned to his native countryside only once, between 1625 and 1627. By the 1630s, his work had matured into one of the most sought after styles in the history of European art. Popes and princes around the world flooded him with commissions. To protect himself from numerous imitators, Claude kept a careful record of his compositions by making drawings in his *Liber Veritatis* between about 1630 and 1678. His popularity never diminished. His tonal approach to natural light and the sensuous qualities of landscape without narrative lie at the fountainhead of the French tradition which continues to flourish through Corot to the Impressionsists.

2. LANDSCAPE WITH A PIPING SHEPHERD
(ca. 1635-1636)
Oil on canvas, 26 x 37-1/2 in. (65.6 x 95.6 cm.)
Signed, lower left: "CLAVDIO IV"

REFERENCES

M. ROTHLISBERGER, "Additions to Claude," *Burlington Magazine*, CX (1968), p. 116, repr. p. 117, Fig. 6.
M. ROTHLISBERGER, "De Bril à Claude," *Revue de l'Art*, (November 1969), no. 5, pp. 57-58, 60; Fig. 14, p. 59.

EXHIBITIONS

London, British Institution, 1828.

COLLECTIONS

W. Sloane Stanley, London (1828);
Earl of Middleton, London (1947);
Private Collection, U.S.A. (1947-1967);
Newhouse Galleries, New York (1967-1969);
The Norton Simon Foundation, Los Angeles (1969).

Louise Moillon

Born about 1610 in Paris; died 1696.

Daughter of Nicolas (d. 1627), who painted portraits and landscapes, and was an active picture dealer. Her brother Isaac (1614-1673) composed tapestry designs for Aubusson, and was one of the first members of the Royal Academy. She was introduced to the formative influence of Flemish still life painting by her step-father, François Garnier (d. 1658), if not also by his colleague Jacques Linard (1600-1645). Inspired by interaction with the many Flemish artists who had been gathering around Saint-Germain-des-Près since the Reign of Henri IV, Linard, Moillon and their circle created a distinctive school of French still life, the qualities of which have yet to be fully appreciated. Her notable contribution and very long career began quite early. Of the approximately 25 works ascribed to her, the earliest is dated 1629 and the last 1682. Her quiet bourgeois life, including marriage to a wood merchant and the raising of children, was not affected by the stylistic changes that took place during the second half of the century. Her style, celebrated by the poet Scudéry in 1646, was the one she achieved in her youth, and the one to which she remained faithful throughout more than fifty years of painting. For her, the lavish decorations that Monnoyer and others painted so flamboyantly at Versailles did not exist. Until the end, she was scrupulously descriptive of precise observation, possessed of exquisite technique, and filled with simple sincerity. In common with the Le Nain brothers (1588-1677) and Georges de la Tour (1593-1652), the selection and treatment of subject matter is much more abstract than the anecdotalists of the Low Countries. Composition is more restrained; tonal harmonies more subtle. The attitude is one of quiet contemplation. This is the spirit to which Chardin would return.

3. STILL LIFE WITH CHERRIES, STRAWBERRIES AND GOOSEBERRIES.
1630
Oil on panel, 12-3/4 x 19-1/4 in. (32.5 x 49 cm.)
Signed and dated, lower left: "Louyse Moillon/ 1630"

REFERENCES
P. WILSON, ed., *Art at Auction* (1971), p. 64, repr. in color.

COLLECTIONS
Owen Grazebrook (sale, Sotheby's, London, 25 November 1970, no. 8, repr.);
Edward Speelman, Ltd., London (by 1972);
The Norton Simon Foundation, Los Angeles (1972).

Jean-Baptiste Monnoyer

Born 1634 in Lille; died 1699.

Began his studies in Antwerp, where he quickly fell into his specialty of flower and fruit still life. Moving to Paris, he was favorably received by Le Brun, who employed him to decorate the residences of Louis XIV including Versailles. He was accepted by the Academy in 1663. In addition to his numerous commissions for architectural decorations, he regularly assisted portrait painters such as Rigaud with floral details. Towards the end of his career he worked in England for Queen Mary and Queen Anne, as well as the owners of large country houses. In the hands of Monnoyer, the history of French still life painting changes direction. The clientele is no longer the *petit bourgeoisie* who enjoy having an attractive, accurate painting on the wall of their small home. The patron is now the King who wants the huge walls of his gigantic palaces filled with opulent symbols of grandeur. Objects once painted for their own sake yielded to being utilized for their decorative value. This impulse towards sumptuous magnificence would culminate in the translation of the work of Monnoyer and his successors into the tapestries of Gobelins.

4. STILL LIFE WITH FLOWERS
Oil on canvas, 29-1/4 x 36 in. (74.2 x 92.6 cm.)

COLLECTIONS
Private Collection (sale, Sotheby's, London, 5 July 1967, no. 74);
Norton Simon Inc. Museum of Art, Los Angeles (5 July 1967).

Nicolas de Largillière

Born 1656 in Paris; died 1746.

Son of a hat-maker, his youth was spent in Antwerp, where he was apprenticed to an obscure painter, and admitted to the Antwerp Guild at the age of sixteen. In 1664 he became the principal assistant of another Flemish artist, Peter Lely (1618-1680), who had succeeded Van Dyck at the English Court. Shortly after Lely's death, Largillière finally returned to Paris in 1682. He was welcomed into the French Royal Academy in 1686 with a masterful portrait of his patron, Charles Le Brun (1619-1690). His audience was new. During the first half of the century, only very few powerful individuals commissioned portraits. Once the religious wars ended, the prestige of family and heredity exerted itself as an even stronger social value than before. During the second half of the century, no upper or middle class home was without a portrait or two. Largillière naturally gravitated to the wealthy bourgeoisie and concentrated his long and distinguished career on portraits of this class, while his friend and rival, Rigaud, focused on the aristocracy. He became a dominant personality in the Academy, and finally its Director from 1738 to 1742. This swelling of the sheer number of patrons increased the quantity of commissioned paintings enormously. Sometimes, as may be seen by the many poor products from Largillière's workshop, the demand outstripped the supply of good work.

5. PIERRE LEPAUTRE. 1689
Oil on canvas, 64-1/4 x 50-3/4 in. (163 x 129 cm.)
Signed and dated, lower center: "N De / Largillière / 1689"

REFERENCES
R. E. SAISSELIN, "The Portrait in History," *Apollo* (October 1963), p. 282, repr.

EXHIBITIONS
Cleveland, Cleveland Museum of Art, "Style, Truth and the Portrait," 2 October-10 November 1963, no. 11.
Milwaukee, Milwaukee Art Center, "The Inner Circle," 15 September-23 October 1966, no. 56.

COLLECTIONS
Scott & Fowles, New York (1911);
William Howard Taft, Cincinnati and Washington, D.C.;
Joseph Levy, New York;
Duveen Galleries, New York (by 1963);
The Norton Simon Foundation, Los Angeles (1964).

REMARKS
The sculptor and engraver Pierre Lepautre (1660-1744) was one of the many talented craftsmen employed by Le Brun to provide decorative sculpture for Versailles and the Tuileries where examples of his work may still be seen.

Hyacinthe Rigaud

Born 1659 in Perpignan; died 1743.

Of a Catalan family, he moved towards Paris slowly, after provincial apprenticeships in Montpellier and Lyons. Once he arrived in Paris, at the age of twenty-one, his success was rapid. He was awarded the *Prix de Rome* in 1682, but was advised by Le Brun to begin his career immediately, rather than travel south. Moreover, like his friend and rival, Largillière, Rigaud's affinity was for the robust qualities of the Flemish Baroque. Although he was frequently opulent, impressing his patrons with sumptuous pomp and masterful artifice, he also could be a very perceptive interpreter of the human face. His masterpieces are of the "Sun King" himself, and of the aristocracy at Court, from the time of Louis XIV, through the Regency, to Louis XV. As the principal official portrait painter, he, necessarily, headed an extremely active studio. His account books indicate that, with the help of numerous assistants, he produced an annual average of 35 portraits for 62 years. Throughout the last decades of the 17th century, and the first decades of the 18th, Largillière and Rigaud dominated French portraiture.

6. NOËL BOUTON, MARQUIS DE CHAMILLY (ca. 1703-1705)
Oil on canvas, 58-1/2 x 45 in.
(148.6 x 114.3 cm.)
Signed, center left: "Fai(t) par Hyacinthe Rigaud"

REFERENCES
H. A. LaFarge, "French Art," *Art News* (November 1952), p. 44.
H. A. LaFarge, "French Seventeenth Century," *Art News* (April 1960), p. 12.
Pictures on Exhibit (March 1961), p. 16, repr. p. 41.

EXHIBITIONS
New York, Duveen Galleries, "French Art in Painting and Sculpture of the Eighteenth Century," October-November 1952, no. 18.
Kansas City, William Rockhill Gallery, "Century of Mozart," 15 January-4 March 1956, no. 91, repr.
Hartford, Wadsworth Atheneum, "Homage to Mozart," 22 March-29 April 1956, no. 49.
New York, Duveen Galleries, "French Seventeenth Century," March-April 1960.
Cleveland, Cleveland Museum of Art, "Style, Truth and the Portrait," 2 October-10 November 1963, no. 19.
London, Royal Academy, "France in the Eighteenth Century," 6 January-3 March 1968, no. 579.

COLLECTIONS
Jules Féral, Paris;
Duveen Galleries, New York (by 1952);
The Norton Simon Foundation, Los Angeles (1964).

REMARKS
Noël Bouton (1636-1715), 3rd Count and 1st Marquis of Chamilly, was a distinguished soldier who became Governor of Graves, Oudernarde and Strasburg, and, in 1703, a Marshal of France.

Jean Antoine Watteau

Born 1684 in Valenciennes; died 1721.

Son of a tiler and carpenter. In his Franco-Flemish town, which officially had become French in 1677, Watteau was exposed to Flemish and Dutch art during his apprenticeship with an obscure genre painter about 1696. In 1702 he moved to Paris, taking employment as a copyist. He then worked under a theatrical painter named Claude Gillot, who seems to have introduced him to the *Commedia dell' arte* about 1704. By 1707 or 1708 Watteau had begun to study with the graceful decorator, Claude Audran III, who was keeper of the collections at the Luxembourg Palace. Regular access to the extraordinary cycle of Rubens there proved to be a continuing source of education and inspiration, as did the remarkable Crozat collection of Venetian paintings and drawings. Although never financially successful, he did become an Associate of the Academy in 1712, and a Member in 1717. The Academy had hesitated in admitting an artist who was doing neither History, Portraiture, Still life, or Genre in the usual sense of actual everyday life. The dream worlds Watteau created did not fit traditional categories. For the work of this delicate poet-painter, a new name—*"fêtes galantes"*—had to be devised for the abstract mood with which he enveloped elegant people amusing themselves in the open air. He would not alter the shape of history much longer. After a brief visit to London in 1719-1720, he died of the tuberculosis with which he had suffered most of his short life. During the next generation all of Europe wished to be inundated with reverberations of his shimmering spirit. His followers and copyists were kept busy in France, England, Portgual, Prussia and Poland. Watteau's work is still widely regarded as the quintessence of French elegance and exquisite sensibility.

7. RECLINING NUDE (ca. 1713-1717)
Oil on panel, 5-1/2 x 6-3/4 in. (14.2 x 17.3 cm.)

REFERENCES

J. MATHEY, *L'Art et Les Artistes* (November 1937), p. 34, repr.
J. MATHEY, "Aspects divers de Watteau dessinateur...", *L'Amour de L'Art* (December 1938), p. 373, repr.
A. M. FRANKFURTER, "383 Masterpieces of Art," *Art News Annual* (May 1940), p. 36, repr.
J. SHAPLEY, "More Masters at the Fair," *Parnassus*, XII (May 1940), pp. 8, 10, repr.
J. MATHEY, *Antoine Watteau: Peintures Réapparues* (1959).
E. CAMESACA, *Complete Paintings of Watteau* (1968), no. 135, repr. p. 109.
D. POSNER, "Watteau's Reclining Nude and the 'Remedy' Theme," *Art Bulletin*, LIX (December 1972), pp. 385-389, repr. in color as frontispiece.

EXHIBITIONS

New York, Knoedler Galleries, "Classics of the Nude," 10 April-6 May 1939, no. 14, repr.
New York, World's Fair, "Masterpieces of Art," 1939, no. 408.
New York, World's Fair, "Masterpieces of Art," May-October 1940, no. 210, repr. p. 143.
Toronto, Toronto Art Gallery, "An Exhibition of Great Paintings," November-December 1940, no. 45, p. 13.

COLLECTIONS

Prince Alexis Orloff, St. Petersburg;
Owen Collection, Paris;
Samuel H. Kress, New York;
Private Collection, Paris;
E. V. Thaw and Co., New York (by 1972);
The Norton Simon Foundation, Los Angeles (1972).

Jean-Baptiste Pater

Born 1695 in Valenciennes; died 1736.

Son of a minor sculptor, who was a friend of Watteau's father. As a fellow townsman, Pater became the only pupil Watteau ever had. The relationship may have started as early as 1710 in Valenciennes, and certainly had begun by 1713 in the Paris studio of the master. The Paris schooling lasted only a few months, owing to the master's extreme irritability. An apologetic Watteau invited him for more meaningful instruction once again for a short period, just before the master's death in 1721. Without the competition of a genius, Pater— along with Nicolas Lancret (1690-1743)—flourished in Watteau's footsteps as popular painters of the *fêtes galantes*. Pater was admitted to the Academy in 1728, and generated a more independent style after 1730.

8. FÊTE GALANTE
Oil on panel, 7-7/8 x 10-3/4 in. (20 x 27.3 cm.)

EXHIBITIONS

Richmond, Virginia Museum of Fine Arts, "Les Fêtes Galantes," 20 January-5 March 1956.

Montreal, Montreal Museum of Fine Arts, "Heritage de France, French Paintings 1610-1760," 6 October-6 November 1961, no. 58, repr.

Quebec, Musée de la Province de Quebec, "Heritage de France, French Paintings 1610-1760," 16 November-16 December 1961.

COLLECTIONS

William, Earl of Lonsdale (sale, Christie's, London, 18 June 1887, no. 886);

Edward Cecil, 1st Earl of Iveagh;

Arthur Earnest Guinness (sale, Christie's, London, 10 July 1953, no. 67);

Arthur Tooth & Sons, London (10 July 1953);

M. Knoelder and Co.;

Valerian Stuy-Rybar (1960-1962);

M. Knoelder and Co. (1963);

Henry T. Mudd, Pasadena (1964);

Richard L. Feigen and Co., New York (by 1970);

The Norton Simon Foundation, Los Angeles (1970).

Maurice Quentin de La Tour

Born 1704 in Saint-Quentin; died 1788.

Son of a musician, whose disapproval of a painter's career led the fifteen-year-old boy to run away from home. After extensive traveling, to London and elsewhere, he settled in Paris during the mid 1720s. Inspired by the popularity of the Venetian pastelist Rosalba Carriera (1675-1757), who visited Paris in 1720-1721, he resolved to show that pastel could hold its own with oil painting. To a remarkable degree he succeeded and became the most celebrated French pastelist of the 18th century, and one of its most penetrating portraitists. His star rose quickly. Lépicié engraved one of his portraits in 1734. Voltaire sat for him in 1736. He was made an associate of the Academy in 1737, and a full Member in 1746. He was a blunt man whose arrogance and high prices were tolerated, even by the King, because of his lively mind and uncanny talent. His work forms perhaps our most faithful visual record of the intimate Rococo *salon,* with all its varied components of spontaneity and superficiality, wit and reason.

9. SELF-PORTRAIT (1764)
Pastel on paper, 17-1/2 x 14-1/2 in.
(44 x 35 cm.)

REFERENCES
A. BESNARD and G. WILDENSTEIN, *Latour, la vie et l'oeuvre de l'artiste* (1928), no. 239.
M. MONDA in *Le Figaro* (31 March 1952).
Time (14 July 1967), p. 64, repr. in color, p. 65.
A. BURY, *Maurice-Quentin de Latour: The Greatest Pastel Portraitist* (1971), opp. pl. 9.

COLLECTIONS
Boitelle (sale, Paris, 24 April 1866, no. 70);
Laperlier, (sale, Paris, 17-18 February 1879, no. 52);
Camille Groult, Paris (by 1952);
A. Costa du Rels, Bolivia, (sale, Sotheby's, London, 5 July 1967, no. 99, repr.);
Robert Ellis Simon, Los Angeles (1967);
The Norton Simon Foundation, Los Angeles (1969).

REMARKS
Latour painted numerous self-portraits, many of which may be found in public collections throughout Europe. The traditional date for this work is given in an inscription on the reverse.

Jean-Baptiste Siméon Chardin

Born 1699 in Paris; died 1779.

Son of a humble cabinetmaker. Apparently encouraged by a sympathetic family, he was enrolled in the traditional craftsmen's guild, the Academy of St. Luke, in 1724. Carefully assimilating lessons from Dutch and Flemish masters, he worked under a series of respectable minor painters. Unlike his more highly paid contemporaries at court, such as Boucher (1703-1770), and Nattier (1685-1766), Chardin was not interested in the "noble" subjects of history and portraiture as such. His audience was the growing French middle class, whose everyday sights and activities were the subject of his gentle perceptions. Methodically developing his extraordinary genius, he gradually became the finest still life and genre painter of 18th century Europe. Sponsored by Largillière, he was elected to the Royal Academy in 1728, serving as its parsimonious Treasurer from 1755, and respected, judicious "curator" of the annual *Salon* for the next twenty years. Eventually, the King granted him a pension and an apartment in the Louvre. His influence on fellow painters was not enormous. Still life remained, as it had been a century before, the least "respectable" of academic subjects. Manet and Cézanne would discover him again.

This pair of paintings is illustrated on the following two pages.

10. & 11. A PAIR OF STILL LIFES
(ca. 1728-1730)
Each, oil on canvas pendant,
15-3/4 x 12-3/8 in. (40 x 31 cm.)
Each signed, lower right: "chardin"

REFERENCES
J. GUIFFREY IN DAYOT, *J. B. Siméon Chardin* (1907), p. 30.
G. WILDENSTEIN, *Chardin* (1933), no. 913, p. 225; no. 943, p. 227; pl. XCII, Figs. 127 & 128.
K. MARTIN, "Notes on a Still Life by Chardin," *Allen Memorial Art Museum Bulletin* (Fall 1951), pp. 20-22, Figs. 1 & 2.
D. WILDENSTEIN, *Chardin* (1969), no. 62 & 63, p. 154, Figs. 29 & 30.
H. FURST, "How to Appreciate Art," *Apollo* (February 1940), p. 33, repr.
H. FURST, "Chardin, Yesterday and Today," *Connoisseur* (19 August 1940), p. 16, repr.
K. MARTIN, "Berwerkungen zu zwei Kopien nach Stolleben von J. B. S. Chardin," *Festschrift (Für) Kurt Bauch* (1957), pp. 238 ff., repr.

EXHIBITIONS
New York, Wildenstein Galleries, "Paintings by J. B. S. Chardin," 1926, nos. 10 & 11, repr.
Paris, Galerie Pigalle, "Exposition Chardin," October 1929, no. 13, repr.
New York, Cultural Division of the French Embassy, "Gastronomy in Fine Arts," 29 November 1951-30 January 1952, nos. 6 & 7.
Houston, Allied Arts Association, "Masterpieces of French Painting through Six Centuries," 16-27 November, 1952 nos. 35 & 36, repr.
Palm Beach, Society of the Four Arts, "Eighteenth Century Masterpieces," 12 December 1952-4 January 1953, nos 5 & 6.
Los Angeles, University of California Art Galleries, "California Collects: North and South," 20 January-23 February 1958, nos. 17 & 18, repr.
San Francisco, California Palace of the Legion of Honor, "California Collects: North and South," 7 March-6 April 1958, nos. 17 & 18, repr.
Los Angeles, University of California Art Galleries, "Rococo to Romanticism," 6 March-16 April 1961, repr.

COLLECTIONS:
MM. Laneuville and Henry, Paris (sale, Paris, 9-11 April 1822, no. 85);
Camille Mareille (1876);
Léon Michel-Levy;
Private Collection, London;
Wildenstein Galleries, Paris (by 1921);
Robert Ellis Simon, Los Angeles (1958);
The Norton Simon Foundation, Los Angeles (1969).

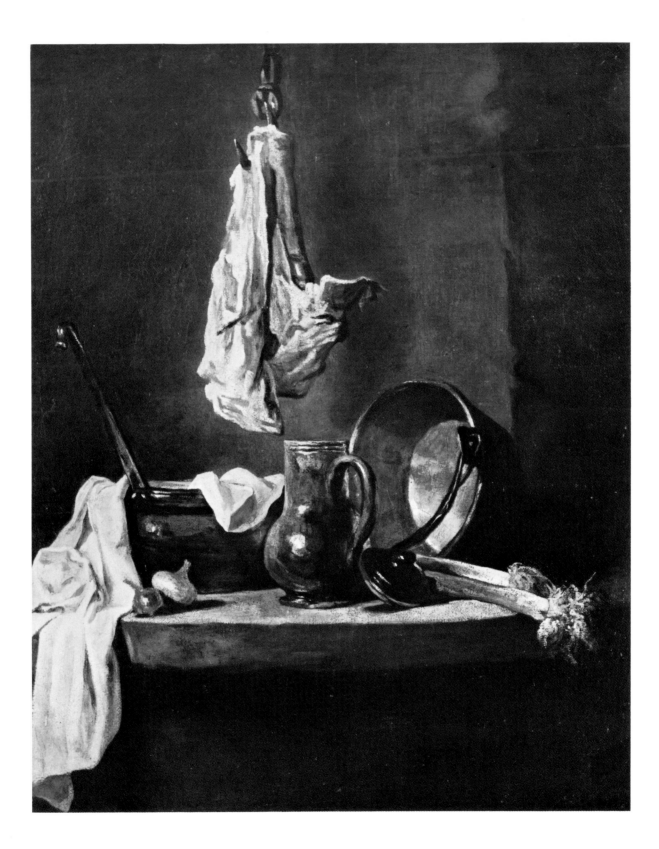

68

Jean Honoré Fragonard

Born 1732 in Grasse; died 1806.

Moved with his family to Paris at about the age of eighteen. He seems to have begun as an apprentice to Chardin for a brief period, then was Boucher's pupil from 1748 to 1752, when he unexpectedly won the *Prix de Rome*. After further training with Carle Van Loo and Lépicié, he went to Rome in 1756. There he became friends with Hubert Robert, and balanced his early affection for northern artists with enthusiasm for Tiepolo. Returning to Paris in 1761, he made a triumphant entry into the Academy in 1765. Many, including Diderot, felt he might be the new hope for French painting which was rapidly losing its vitality. That he proved to be, and more, as an individual. But his influence was not wide-spread. Although he enjoyed royal patronage, from Madame de Pompadour and Madame Dubarry, Fragonard preferred to work privately, outside the psychological restrictions of the Court and the Academy. Surprisingly, the Revolution did not alter his fortunes immediately. In 1791 his friend David appointed him Curator of the Louvre for four years. But the smell of aristocracy hovered around his head. He was forced from his apartment in the Louvre, and deprived of his pension. He died impoverished and forgotten. Fragonard's reputation has suffered from too close an association with the perfumed decorations of Boucher. Not only did he feel humanity much more deeply, but his ability to handle paint has seldom, if ever, been exceeded. Daumier and Renoir revered this painter's painter—Fragonard of the fiery brush.

12. & 13. VENUS BINDING CUPID'S WINGS and MUSIC (ca. 1760-1765)
Each oil on canvas over-door pendant, 30-3/4 x 52 in. (78 x 132 cm.)

REFERENCES
G. WILDENSTEIN, *The Paintings of Fragonard* (1960), no. 51 bis, p. 204, Fig. 35 bis., no. 51 ter, p. 205, Fig. 36 bis.

COLLECTIONS
Mme. M. Ephrussi;
Private Collection, France;
Galerie André Weil, Paris (by 1969);
The Norton Simon Foundation, Los Angeles (1969).

REMARKS
An oil sketch of *Venus Binding Cupid's Wing* (Wildenstein No. 52, Fig. 34) from the collection of Major Hugh Rose, was sold at Sotheby's 6 December 1967, no. 15.

This pair of paintings is illustrated on the following two pages.

14. THE CAGE or THE HAPPY LOVERS

(ca. 1760-1765)

Oil on canvas, 35-1/2 x 47 in. (90.2 x 119.4 cm.)

REFERENCES

L. MERRICK, "Fragonard's Graceful Art," *American Art News*
(24 January 1914), p. 3.
A. VAN CLEEF, "The Fragonard Show," *American Art News*
(31 January 1914), p. 6.
Art News (18 May 1940), p. 13, repr.
Art Digest (1 April 1945), p. 7, repr.
"Old Masters Feature Flint Victory Show," *Art Digest*
(15 September 1945), p. 8.
"Fifteenth Anniversary Exhibition," *Springfield Museum of Fine
Arts Bulletin*, XV (October-November 1948), p. 3
L. REAU, *Fragonard, Sa vie et son oeuvre* (1956), p. 160.
G. WILDENSTEIN, *The Paintings of Fragonard* (1960), no. 31,
p. 199, Fig. 24.
New York Times Magazine (12 February 1961), repr.

EXHIBITIONS

New York, Gimpel & Wildenstein Galleries, "Paintings &
Drawings by Fragonard," 1914, no. 26.
New York, Metropolitan Museum of Art, "Jules Bache
Collection," Summer 1940.
Toronto, Art Gallery of Toronto, "Exhibition of Great
Paintings," 1940, no. 49.
Buffalo, Albright Art Gallery, "European Paintings of the
15th, 16th, 17th and 18th Centuries," March-April 1942,
repr.
Flint, Flint Institute of Arts, "Paintings by Old Masters,"
1945, no. 10, repr.
Detroit, Detroit Institute of Arts, "French Paintings of the
XVII-XXth Centuries," 6-30 March 1947, no. 159.
Springfield, Museum of Fine Arts, "Fifteenth Anniversary
Exhibition," October-November 1948, repr.
New York, Duveen Galleries, "French Art in Painting and
Sculpture of the Eighteenth Century," October-November
1952, no. 4.
London (Ontario), University of Western Ontario, "17th-18th
Century French Masters," February-March 1953, repr.
Houston, The Museum of Fine Arts, "George Washington's
World," 16 January-14 February 1954, no. 159.
New York, Duveen Galleries, "Halcyon Days," May 1959.
Los Angeles, U.C.L.A. Art Galleries, "Rococo to
Romanticism," March-April 1961, repr. in color, p. 6.
London, Royal Academy, "France in the Eighteenth Century,"
6 January-3 March 1968, no. 226.

COLLECTIONS

Hippolyte Poitevin, Paris;
Gimpel and Wildenstein Galleries, New York;
Judge Elbert H. Gary, New York (by 1927);
Mrs. Lewis Nixon, New York;
Duveen Galleries, New York (by 1940);
The Norton Simon Foundation, Los Angeles (1964).

Jean Auguste Dominique Ingres

Born 1780 in Montauban; died 1867

Son of a decorative sculptor from Toulouse. There, as a youth, Ingres studied with followers of David whose studio he entered at the age of sixteen in 1796. He won the *Prix de Rome* in 1801, but remained in Paris, where he painted a series of magnificent portraits in the full maturity of his genius. In 1806 he went to Italy where he stayed for eighteen years; married happily; and created a stylistic synthesis out of the influences of the classical Raphael and the manneristic Pontormo and Bronzino. For some time it was necessary that he support himself with portraits and portrait drawings of wealthy tourists. But what he preferred to do were sensuous studies of the female nude. The work he sent to the *Salons* established him as the hero of the powerful majority who were opposed to Delacroix. The old debate between the *Poussinistes* and the *Rubénsistes* continued throughout the lifetimes of these two great painters who could bring themselves to speak with one another only once. Ingres returned to Paris in 1824, founded a school of more than a hundred students, and received all the official honors France could bestow—from the presidency of the *École des Beaux-Arts*; to the directorship of the French Academy in Rome from 1834 to 1841 (when he returned again to Paris); and the distinguished office of senator in 1862. His brilliance continued through the very last years of his long life. His most famous masterpiece, *The Turkish Bath* (Louvre, Paris), was completed when he was eighty-three. During the second half of the 19th century, almost all of the Academy followed the example of Ingres, while almost all of the revolutionary painters followed the example of Delacroix. Only one artist, Degas, managed to create a synthesis from the best of both traditions.

15. ODALISQUE WITH SLAVE. 1839

Pencil, black chalk and white gouache with gray and brown wash on cream wove paper on thinner secondary sheet, 13-1/8 x 18-1/4 in. (33.3 x 46.4 cm.)
Signed and dated, lower left:
"J. Ingres/Rom. 1839"

REFERENCES

Petit Palais, Paris, *Ingres* (1968), p. 268, note.
E. RADIUS, *L'Opera Completa di Ingres* (1968), p. 107, no. 128, note.
Fogg Art Museum, Cambridge, *Greenville L. Winthrop: Retrospective for a Collector* (1969), p. 116, no. 85, note.

EXHIBITIONS

Philadelphia, Philadelphia Museum of Art, "The Hanley Collection," 1957.
Hartford, Wadsworth Atheneum, "Paintings and Drawings from the Hanley Collection," 1961, no. 77.
New York, Wildenstein and Co., "Paintings and Drawings from the Hanley Collection," 22 November-30 December, 1961, no. 77.
Cambridge, Fogg Art Museum, "Paintings and Drawings from the Hanley Collection," 24 January-15 April 1962, no. 77.
New York, Gallery of Modern Art, "Selections from the Collection of Dr. and Mrs. T. Edward Hanley," 3 January-12 March 1967, no. 32, repr.
Philadelphia, Philadelphia Museum of Art, "Selections from the Collection of Dr. and Mrs. T. Edward Hanley," 6 April-28 May 1967, no. 32, repr.
Midland, Texas, Museum of the Southwest, "Selections from the Collection of Dr. and Mrs. T. Edward Hanley," 1967, no. 93.
Denver, The Denver Art Museum, "Selections from the Collection of Dr. and Mrs. T. Edward Hanley," 1967, no. 93.
San Francisco, M. H. de Young Memorial Museum, "Selections from the Collection of Dr. and Mrs. T. Edward Hanley," 24 November 1967-2 February 1968, no. 93.
Columbus, Columbus Gallery of Fine Arts, "Works from the Hanley Collection," 7 November-15 December, 1969, no. 79.

COLLECTIONS

Gustave Periere, Paris;
Georges Seligman, New York;
Dr. and Mrs. T. Edward Hanley, Bradford, Pennsylvania (by 1957);
E. V. Thaw and Co., New York (by 1969);
The Norton Simon Foundation, Los Angeles (1969).

REMARKS

This drawing seems to be a study for the painting of the same title in the Fogg Art Museum, Cambridge, Massachusetts. Both works bear an identical inscription. A later version of the Fogg painting, dated 1842, is in the Walters Art Gallery in Baltimore. Until the question has been thoroughly studied, the possibility should not be excluded that this drawing may be intermediary between the two versions.

Ferdinand Victor Eugène Delacroix

Born 1798 in Charenton-Saint-Maurice; died 1863.

Possibly the natural son of the powerful statesman Talleyrand (1754-1838). He was able to study the extraordinary collection Napoleon had assembled from the capitals of Europe until they were returned in 1815. About that time, he entered the studio of Guérin (1774-1833), a follower of David, who also had been the master of Géricault (1791-1824). He was devoted to Michelangelo and Rubens; and was influenced by Gros (1771-1835) and Géricault. He was also a friend of Bonington, and admired Gainsborough, Constable and Turner, especially after his visit to London in 1825. In 1822 his first *Salon* entry, *The Bark of Dante* (Louvre, Paris), immediately placed him in the forefront of the Romantic movement, of which he became the undisputed leader on the early death of his friend Géricault in 1824. For the next quarter century French artists would argue over which towering genius to follow—Ingres and line, or Delacroix and color. Delacroix's color would eventually win, but not the rest of his art. Like all great artists, he was both a conclusion and a starting point. He was the last important muralist, and (although not a practicing Christian) the last significant religious painter in the traditional sense. Almost all his subjects were literary. The "real life" would become the exclusive subject matter of his successors. But they would look at it through his eyes, in one degree or another, from the Barbizon School, and the Impressionists, to Post-Impressionists, Expressionists and Fauves. Few had the privilege of being intimate with him. Chopin and George Sand were exceptions. The rest of Paris only saw a living legend walking through the streets, or like Monet caught a glimpse of him working in his garden, focusing his inexhaustible energy on one of 12,000 canvases. His *Journal* would have made him famous, even if he had never painted.

16. ABD ER RAHMAN, THE SULTAN OF MOROCCO REVIEWING HIS GUARD. 1856

Oil on canvas, 25-1/2 x 21-1/2 in. (65 x 55 cm.)

Signed and dated, lower right: "Eug. Delacroix 1856"

REFERENCES

A. ROBAUT, *L'Oeuvre Complet de Eugene Delacroix, Peintures, Dessins, Gravures, Lithographies* (1885), no. 1295, repr.

EXHIBITIONS

Paris, "Exposition du Centenaire de l'Algérie," 1930.

COLLECTIONS

F. Hartman (sale, Paris, May 1881);
M. G. Pereire;
Mir;
Private Collection, France;
Hector Brame, S.A., Paris (by 1972);
The Norton Simon Foundation, Los Angeles (1972).

REMARKS

The scene, which Delacroix witnessed in 1832, was the subject of at least three very similar oils and a number of drawings from that year until the last version in 1862.

Honoré Daumier

Born 1808 in Marseilles; died 1879.

Son of a picture-framer with literary interests who brought his family to Paris in 1816. After working for a bailiff and a bookstore, he entered the studio of Alexandre Lenoir and, later, the *Académie Suisse*. Of the masters he copied in the Louvre he was most deeply impressed by the monumental figure-style of Rubens, the spontaneous technique of Fragonard, and the raw, emotional realities of Goya. By 1822 he had learned lithography from Ramelet, and soon began his long career as a masterful creator of caricature. Most of his 4,000 prints were published weekly in *La Caricature,* which was edited by Balzac, and *Le Charivari* between 1830 and 1872. As one of the finest draftsmen of his century, his graphic work transcends the usual limits of illustration. He delineated a portrait of his age at a level of complexity and completeness that Hogarth and Rowlandson only begin to approach. His humanity was enormous. The intensity of his invective against the repressive regime of Louis Philippe was more than the government could tolerate. In 1831 Daumier found himself in prison for six months, where he began to paint. Unfortunately, painting was a luxury he could afford only at odd moments between print-making. Although the full greatness of his potential could not be realized under these circumstances, he did become the only major painter of his time to develop totally outside the Academy and the *Salon.* During the calmer years of the Third Republic, Daumier painted more and became friends with Diaz, Millet, Daubigny and Corot, who saved him from poverty when he became a blind old man after 1872. His first exhibition was not held until 1878. His work exerted a distinct influence on Munch, Rouault, and German Expressionists. What little survives of his original sculpture is suggestive of the freedom that Rodin would later bring to three-dimensional form.

17. MOUNTEBANKS RESTING
(ca. 1865-1866)
Oil on canvas, 11-1/2 x 14-1/2 in.
(29.2 x 36.8 cm.)

REFERENCES
D. PHILLIPS, *A Collection Still in the Making,* 1927, pl. XIV, repr.
E. FUCHS, *Der Maler Daumier* (1930), repr. p. 300.
K. MAISON, *Honoré Daumier, Catalogue Raisonné of Paintings, Watercolours and Drawings* (1968), no. II-43, repr. pl. 196.

EXHIBITIONS
Paris, Galerie Georges Petit, "Daumier," 1908.
New York, Knoedler Galleries, "The Remarque Collection," 1943, no. 4, repr.
Los Angeles, Los Angeles County Museum of Art, "Honoré Daumier," 1958, no. 220.

COLLECTIONS
Colonel Briggs;
Duncan Phillips, Washington, D.C.;
S. Salz, New York;
Erich Maria Remarque;
19th and 20th Century Art, Inc., New York (by 1957);
Robert Ellis Simon, Los Angeles (1957);
The Norton Simon Foundation, Los Angeles (1969).

REMARKS
Daumier often painted several versions of the same subject at different times, often years apart. Until the chronology of Daumier's work has been more clearly established, it will not be certain whether this painting is earlier or later than the following version.

18. MOUNTEBANKS RESTING

(ca. 1865-1866)
Oil on canvas, 21-1/4 x 26 in. (54 x 66 cm.)
Signed, lower left: "h. Daumier".

REFERENCES

G. GEFFROY, *Daumier* (1901), repr., pl. facing p. 20.

L. ROSENTHAL, *Daumier* (n.d.), cat. p. 85, repr. pl. 12.

M. SACHS, *Honoré Daumier* (n.d.), op. 23, repr. pl. 12.

A. SOFFICI, "Daumier Pittore" *Dedalo* (November 1921), repr. p. 415.

D. PHILLIPS, *Honoré Daumier* (1922).

R. ESCHOLIER, *Daumier* (1923), repr. opp. p. 8.

A. FONTAINAS, *La Peinture de Daumier* (1923), repr. pl. 23 as "Au Cabaret."

E. KLOSSOWSKI, *Honoré Daumier* (1923), p. 104, no. 204, repr. pl. 84.

M. SADLEIR, *Daumier, the Man and the Artist* (1924), pp. 33-34, repr. pl. 9.

Art News (22 January 1927), repr. p. 10.

A. FONTAINAS, *Daumier* (1927).

A. ALEXANDRE, *Daumier* (1928), repr. pl. 33.

J. MEIER-GRAEFE, "Honoré Daumier Fifty Years After," *International Studio* (September 1929), repr. in color opp. p. 21.

American Magazine of Art (December 1930), p. 707.

E. FUCHS, *Der Maler Daumier* (1930), p. 51, no. 131, repr. p. 131.

Formes (December 1931), repr. opp. p. 185.

Art News (9 January 1932), repr. p. 5.

G. WILDENSTEIN, "Paintings from America in the French Exhibition," *Fine Arts* (January 1932), repr. p. 25.

R. ESCHOLIER, *Daumier* (1932), repr. following p. 40.

B. FLEISCHMANN, *Honoré Daumier* (1938), repr. pl. 12.

J. LASSAIGNE, *Daumier* (1938), p. 168, repr. pl. 146.

Pacific Art Review (1944), p. 22.

M. GAUTHIER, *Daumier* (1950), repr. pl. 57.

C. SCHWEICHER, *Daumier* (1953), repr. pl. 10.

J. ADHEMAR, *Honoré Daumier* (1954) p. 129, no. 160, repr. pl. 160 and in color on cover.

K. MAISON, *Honoré Daumier, Catalogue Raisonné of Paintings, Watercolours, and Drawings* (1968), no. I-185, repr. pl. 136.

EXHIBITIONS

Paris, École des Beaux-Arts, "Exposition Daumier," May 1901, p. 19, no. 62.

New York, The Museum of Modern Art, "Corot-Daumier," 16 October-23 November 1930, no. 72, repr.

London, Burlington House, "Royal Academy Exhibition of French Art 1200-1900," 1932, p. 194, no. 410; *Commemorative Catalogue*, 1933, p. 80, no. 330.

New York, The Metropolitan Museum of Art, "Taste of Today in Masterpieces of Painting," 1932.

New York, Durand-Ruel Galleries, "Great French Masters of the Nineteenth Century," 12 February-10 March 1934, repr. no. 12.

Paris, Musée de l'Orangerie, "Exposition Daumier," 1934, p. 69, no. 35.

Philadelphia, Pennsylvania Museum of Art, "Daumier," 1937, pp. 22-23, no. 8, repr.

Los Angeles, Los Angeles County Museum of Art, "Honoré Daumier" 1958, no. 221.

COLLECTIONS

Durand-Ruel, Paris;

Jean Joubert;

Paul Rosenberg, Paris;

C. C. Stillman, (sale, New York, Feb. 1927, no. 23);

Arthur Sachs, Paris and New York;

Wildenstein and Co., Inc., New York;

Norton Simon, Los Angeles (1955).

20. REBECCA AT THE WELL. 1839

Oil on canvas, 19-5/8 x 29-1/8 in. (50 x 74 cm.)
Signed and dated, lower right: "Corot 1839"

REFERENCES

A. ROBAUT, *L'Oeuvre de Corot* (1905), no. 382, repr.

EXHIBITIONS

Paris, Galerie Rosenberg, "Corot: Figures et paysages
   d'Italie," 1928, no. 20.
Paris, Musée de l'Orangerie, "Corot," 1936, no. 36,
   repr. pl. IV.
Paris, Galerie Schmit, "Corot," 1971, no. 13, repr. in color.

COLLECTIONS

Chailloux;
Manzi;
Gallimard;
Jules Strauss, (sale, Paris, 3 May 1902, no. 12, repr.);
Hazard, (sale, Paris, 1-3 December 1919, no. 75, repr.);
David-Weil, Paris;
Galerie Schmit, Paris (by 1972);
The Norton Simon Foundation, Los Angeles (1972).

Charles François Daubigny

Born 1817 in Paris; died 1878.

Son of a minor landscape painter who worked in the classical style of Bertin. At the age of seventeen he visited Italy, after which he earned his living as an illustrator, decorator of candy boxes, and a restorer at the Louvre. After a brief, unprofitable study with Delaroche, he started to exhibit at the *Salon* in 1838. He received a second-class medal at the liberalizing *Salon* of 1848, and a first-class in 1853 when Louis Napoleon bought one his paintings. He seems to have been the only member of the Barbizon group who worked directly and completely from nature. As early as 1857, he constructed a floating studio in a rowboat, which he called "Le Botin." The principal reason he was not more of a popular success is that he was working in a spontaneous, tonal style which anticipates Impressionism. In 1861 Gautier observed that Daubigny is satisfied with only "an impression. . . . His pictures are but rough drafts, . . . very slightly developed . . . merely spots of color juxtaposed." In 1865 another critic dubbed him "chief of the school of the impression." Monet was deeply influenced by this way of trying to capture the ever fluctuating aspects of nature. In 1856, when Monet had very little money to spare, he bought a Daubigny. Monet also was to pursue Daubigny's (and Jongkind's) idea of painting the same subject under different conditions of light and weather, and built a floating studio to help him to get "closer" to nature. In both style and personality Daubigny forms a link between two important generations. Guests on his boat included not only Corot, Daumier, Barye and Courbet, but Pissarro and Cézanne from the *Académie Suisse*. The cycle of influence became complete when Daubigny and Monet became friends in London during 1870-1871. From then on Monet's lighter palette and brush stroke find themselves reflected in the work of the man who had been the inspiration of his youth.

21. DAY BREAK. 1869
   Oil on canvas, 32-3/4 x 57-1/8 in.
   (83.2 x 45 cm.)
   Signed and dated, lower left: "Daubigny 1869"

COLLECTIONS
The Duke of Westminster;
Arthur Tooth and Sons, London (by 1964);
The Norton Simon Foundation, Los Angeles (1964).

Gustave Courbet

Born 1819 in Ornans; died 1877

Son of a prosperous landowner who sent him to school in Ornans and Besançon, until he finally received permission to go to Paris at the age of twenty. He quickly became friends with artists, and began to study with an academic painter. Rejecting both polarities in the tradition of Romantic Classicism, he began to work out his own ideas at the *Académie Suisse*, where models were provided but no instruction given. He also spent a great deal of time in museums being particularly impressed with Dutch and Spanish painters. Courbet rapidly came to the conclusion that an artist should paint only what can actually be seen, and that as it is seen without symbolic embellishment or sentimentality. "Show me an angel and I will paint one," he said. After being continually refused by the *Salon*, his masterpieces began to receive gold medals in the liberalized exhibitions that followed the Revolution of 1848. From then on he was the most conspicuous leader of the revolt against the Academy. He regularly enjoyed a *"succès du scandale"* at each of the *Salons*. In 1853 the Emperor threatened to attack one of his canvases with a whip. His position as *chef d'école* was firmly established at the *Exposition Universalle* of 1855, where he had the audacity to set up an exhibition of his work that the jury had rejected, accompanied by a manifesto of "Realism." For two decades he probably was the most talked about artist in Paris. His years of success and prosperity were ended by the Franco-Prussian War. In 1870 Courbet (long an outspoken critic of the government from which he refused the Legion of Honor), became a member of the socialist *Commune*, which attempted to gain political control of Paris. In his official position, Courbet voted for the destruction of the Vendôme column, a monument to Napoleon I. After the bloody defeat of the *Commune*, the new government held Courbet responsible for the column's ruin. He was jailed for six months, and fined a huge sum to replace the monument. Unable to pay, and fearing further imprisonment, he fled in 1873 to Switzerland where he died. The extraordinary strength of his personality, as a painter and as a person, was a primary influence on the Impressionist generation. Courbet's historical position, summarizing as it does much of what had taken place within the Naturalistic movement, and anticipating what would follow, is so important that it can be thought of as the fulcrum of French art at mid-century.

22. SEASCAPE (ca. 1866)

Oil on canvas, 19-3/4 x 24 in. (50 x 61 cm.)
Signed, lower left: "Gustave Courbet"

EXHIBITIONS
Bristol, City Art Gallery, "From a Private Collection," 1968, no. 20.

COLLECTIONS
Jacques Dubourg, Paris;
Roland, Browse and Delbanco, London (1953);
R. C. Pritchard (1954);
E. V. Thaw and Co., New York (by 1970);
The Norton Simon Foundation, Los Angeles (1970).

23. THE STREAM OF THE PUITS-NOIR AT ORNANS (1868)

Oil on canvas, 39 x 59 in. (98.7 x 150 cm.)

Signed and inscribed, lower left: "G. Courbet
Ruisseau du Puits-Noir à Ornans"

REFERENCES

P. CASSIRER, *Schmeil Sammlung* (1916), repr. pl. 8.
J. MEIER-GRAEFE, *Courbet* (1921), repr. p. 32.

COLLECTIONS

Duke of Wagram (by 1906);
Galerie Georges Petit, Paris (1906);
Heinemann Gallery, Munich (1908);
Schmeil, Dresden (sale, Paul Cassirer Gallery, Berlin,
    17 October 1916);
Paul Kantor Gallery, Beverly Hills (by 1965);
Norton Simon, Los Angeles (1965).

24. CLIFF AT ETRETAT, LA PORTE d'AVAL. 1869

Oil on canvas, 25-3/4 x 32 in. (65 x 81 cm.)

Signed and dated, lower right: "G. Courbet '69"

REFERENCES

G. Riat, *Gustave Courbet, Peintre* (1906), p. 268.

J. Laran and P. Gaston-Dreyfus, *Gustave Courbet, Precedé d'une un étude biographique et critique par Léonce Bénédite* (1911), pp. 97-98, repr. pl. XLI.

J. Laran and P. Gaston-Dreyfus, *Gustave Courbet with a Biographical and Critical Study by Léonce Bénédite* (1913), pp. 81-82, repr. pl. XLI.

EXHIBITIONS

Paris, Galerie Alfred Daber, "Courbet, Exposition du 130 anniversaire de sa naissance," June 1949, no. 16, repr.

New York, Paul Rosenberg & Co., "Gustave Courbet," 16 January-11 February 1956, no. 16, repr.

Philadelphia, Philadelphia Museum of Art, "Gustave Courbet," 1959, no. 73, repr.

Boston, Museum of Fine Arts, "Gustave Courbet," 1960, no. 73, repr.

COLLECTIONS

Duc de Trévise, Paris;

Galerie Alfred Daber, Paris (1949);

Paul Rosenberg & Co., New York (by 1950);

R. Sturgis Ingersoll, Penllyn, Pa., (1950);

Jane Wade, Ltd., New York (1969);

The Norton Simon Foundation, Los Angeles (1969).

REMARKS

Courbet painted this subject from several different points of view during 1868-1869. The best known of this series is in the Louvre.

25. STILL LIFE: APPLES, PEARS AND PRIMROSES ON A TABLE. 1871

Oil on canvas, 23-1/2 x 28-3/4 in.
   (59.6 x 73 cm.)

Signed, inscribed and dated, lower right:
   "St. Pelagie / G. Courbet '71"

REFERENCES

D. S. MacColl, *Nineteenth Century Art* (1902), repr. opp. p. 146.
A. J. M. Reid, "Courbet Paintings in Scotland," *Scottish Art Review*, III (1962), repr. p. 31.

EXHIBITIONS

Glasgow, "Loan Exhibition in Aid of the Royal Infirmary," 1878, no. 135.
Edinburgh, "International Exhibition," 1886, no. 1136.
Glasgow, "International Exhibition," 1888, no. 746.
Glasgow, "International Exhibition," 1901.
London, Marlborough Fine Art Galleries, "A Great Period of French Painting," June-July 1963, no. 7, repr.
Glasgow, Scottish Arts Council, "A Man of Influence: Alex Reid 1854-1928," Summer 1967, no. 18.
London, Reid & Lefevre Gallery, "XIX and XX Century French Paintings," November-December 1968, no. 10, repr. in color.

COLLECTIONS

W. Craike Angus, Glasgow;
J. G. Sandeman;
T. G. Arthur;
Ian MacNicol, Glasgow;
Private Collection, Scotland;
Alex Reid and Lefevre Ltd., London (by 1968);
Paul Rosenberg & Co., New York (by 1969);
The Norton Simon Foundation, Los Angeles (1969).

26. HENRI ROCHEFORT (1874)

Oil on canvas, 26-1/2 x 21 in.
(67.3 x 53.3 cm.)
Signed, lower left: "G. Courbet"

REFERENCES

G. RIAT. *Gustave Courbet, Peintre* (1906), p. 356, no. 72
  repr. p. 283.
J. MEIER-GRAEFE, *Courbet* (1921) repr. pl. 114.
C. LEGER, *Courbet* (1929), p. 202, repr. p. 195.
C. LEGER, *Courbet et son temps* (*Lettres et Documents inédits*),
  1948, p. 165.

EXHIBITIONS

Bern, Kunstmuseum, 1962, no. 82.

COLLECTIONS

Durand-Ruel, Paris;
O. Gerstenberg, Berlin;
Paul Rosenberg & Co., New York (by 1972);
The Norton Simon Foundation, Los Angeles (1972).

REMARKS

Henri Rochefort, Marquis de Rochefort-Luçay (1830-1913)
was a radical writer and publisher, who was imprisoned and
exiled on numerous occasions for his political views. His
famous prison escape from New Caledonia in 1874 brought
him through San Francisco. Sympathetically admired by
many artists of his era, he also was portrayed by Manet and
Rodin.

Henri Fantin-Latour

Born 1836 in Grenoble; died 1904.

Son of a Russian mother and a French painter who gave him his first training. Moving to Paris, he spent a great deal of time copying at the Louvre, and was fundamentally influenced by Courbet with overtones derived from Delacroix. He exhibited regularly at the *Salon* from 1861, and declined to exhibit with the Impressionists. That decision seems appropriate. Although he was friendly with the most progressive artists of his day, from Manet to Whistler, and participated in their famous discussions at the Café Guerbois, their stylistic innovations did not suit his own attitude towards painting. His famous group portraits in the Louvre, conceived in the spirit of Courbet, are very interesting social documents. The *Homage to Delacroix* was done just after the master's death in 1864. By 1870, the man in the middle of Fantin's picture, and at the center of the pivotal change in the history of French painting is Manet, around whom are Monet, Renoir, Bazille, and probably would have been Pissarro and Sisley had they been in Paris for a sitting. His best loved work, flower pieces, are a sensitive synthesis of traditional restraint and coloration of such vibrance it sometimes suggests the intensity usually associated with Symbolism.

27. WHITE AND PINK MALLOWS IN A VASE. (1895)
Oil on canvas, 21-1/8 x 19-5/8 in.
(53.5 x 49.7 cm.)
Signed, lower right: "Fantin"

REFERENCES
V. FANTIN-LATOUR, *Catalogue de l'Oeuvre Complet de Fantin-Latour* (1911 and 1969), no. 1595.
M. WYKES-JOYCE, "Fantin-Latour's Flowers," *Amateur Artist* (August 1966), p. 12, repr. in color.

EXHIBITIONS
New York, Acquavella Galleries, "Flowers by Fantin-Latour," 2 November-3 December 1966, no. 18, repr. in color.

COLLECTIONS
Mrs. Edwin Edwards (Acquired from the artist);
Heseltine (by 1911);
J. B. Bennett and Son, Glasgow;
William A. Cargill, Carruth, Bridge of Weir, Scotland, (sale, Sotheby's, London, June 11, 1963, no. 25, repr. in color);
Acquavella Galleries, New York (by 1966);
The Norton Simon Foundation, Los Angeles (1967).

Édouard Manet

Born 1832 in Paris; died 1883.

Son of an affluent official of the Ministry of Justice, who encouraged him to try the navy, before reluctantly permitting him to study under Thomas Couture (1815-1879) in 1850. Unsympathetic with this master's narrowly academic attitude, but intensely interested in learning from the Old Masters, the ambivalent Manet stayed with Couture for seven years. Most of his education, however, took place during his extensive travels, and while copying at the Louvre. By the early 1860s he had assimilated all he needed from Velázquez, Goya, Giorgone, Titian, Hals, Rubens, Delacroix, as well as Japanese prints and photographs. Throughout the decade he proceeded to revolutionize French painting with such works as *Luncheon on the Grass*, from the 1863 *Salon des Refusés*, and *Olympia* from the 1865 *Salon*. His position as "leader" of the avant-garde was consolidated by the one-man show he set up privately beside the pavilion of a jealous Courbet at the World's Fair of 1867. About 1869 his friend Berthe Morisot (who later became his sister-in-law) opened him to more Impressionistic influences. And in 1874 Monet finally persuaded him to try painting out-of-doors. Although he may have been most at ease with Baudelaire, Mallarmé, and Zola, he was friendly with Monet, Renoir, Pissarro and Sisley, and Degas, and certainly influenced all of them. But he thought of himself as liberal rather than radical, and did not like being publicly described as the leader of "Manet's gang." Continuing to hope for official recognition from the *Salon*, he refused to participate in the anti-academic Impressionist exhibitions. Near the end of his life, when Impressionism had begun to influence the Academy, he finally was given the Legion of Honor.

28. MADAME MANET (1866)

Oil on canvas: 24 x 19-1/2 in. (61 x 49.5 cm.)
Stamped, lower right: "Ed. Manet"

REFERENCES

E. ZOLA, *Édouard Manet: Étude biographique et critique* (1867), p. 37.
T. DURET, *Histoire d'Édouard Manet et de son oeuvre* (1902), p. 37.
E. MOREAU-NELATON, *Catalogue manuscrit de l'oeuvre de Manet* (1906), preserved in the Bibliothèque Nationale, no. 106.
J. MEIER-GRAEFE, *Édouard Manet* (1912), p. 222, Fig. 125.
E. WALDMANN, "Leibl und die Französen," *Kunst und Kunstler*, XII (October 1913), pp. 43, 52.
E. MOREAU-NELATON, *Manet*, I (1926), repr. Fig. 114, opp. p. 199.
T. DURET, *Manet* (1926), p. 249, no. 105.
A. TABARANT, *Manet* (1931), p. 161, no. 120.
P. JAMOT and G. WILDENSTEIN, *Manet* (1932), I, no. 144; II, Fig. 163.
A. TABARANT, *Manet et ses oeuvres* (1947), pp. 80, 129-130, 134, repr. p. 606, Fig. 123.

EXHIBITIONS

Paris, "Place de l'Alma," 1867, no. 14.
Dublin, "Art Loan Exhibition," 1899.
London, New Burlington Galleries, "Masters of French 19th Century Painting," October 1936, no. 35.
London, The National Gallery, "Nineteenth Century French Paintings," February-March 1943, no. 14.
Detroit, Detroit Institute of Arts, "The Two Sides of the Medal," 1954, p. 15, no. 19, repr. p. 12.
Philadelphia, Philadelphia Museum of Art, "Édouard Manet," 3 November-11 December 1966, no. 103, repr.
Chicago, The Art Institute of Chicago, "Édouard Manet," 13 January-19 February 1967.

COLLECTIONS

George Moore, London (given to Mr. Moore by Manet);
Lady Cunard (bequest of Mr. Moore);
Sir Robert Abdy (bequest of Lady Cunard);
Wildenstein and Co., New York (by 1956);
Norton Simon, Los Angeles (1956).

29. THE RAGPICKER (ca. 1869)

Oil on canvas, 76-3/4 x 51-1/4 in.
(195 x 130 cm.)
Signed, lower right: "Manet"

REFERENCES

T. Duret, *Histoire d'Édouard Manet et de son oeuvre* (1902), no. 95, p. 70.

E. Moreau-Nelaton, *Catalogue manuscrit de l'oeuvre de Manet*, (1906), preserved in the Bibliothèque Nàtionále, no. 117.

J. Meier-Graefe, *Édouard Manet* (1912), Fig. 48.

T. Duret, *Manet and the French Impressionists* (1910), no. 95, p. 224.

T. Duret, *Manet and the French Impressionists* (1912), no. 95, p. 228.

E. Waldmann, *Édouard Manet* (1923), pp. 35 & 46.

E. Moreau-Nelaton, *Manet raconté par lui-méme* (1926), I, no. 44, p. 109, Fig. 121; II, pp. 47 & 128, Fig. 339.

F. Watson, "Adolphe Lewisohn Collection," *The Arts* (1926), p. 31, repr. p. 18.

T. Duret, *Histoire d'Édouard Manet et son Oeuvre* (1926), no. 95, p. 248.

S. Bourgeois, *The Adolphe Lewisohn Collection of Modern French Painting and Sculpture* (1928), p. 67, repr.

L. Venturi, "Manet," *L'Arte* (1929), p. 154.

A. Tabarant, *Manet* (1931), no. 186, pp. 146-147.

P. Jamot and G. Wildenstein, *Manet* (1932), no. 153, I, pp. 89 & 137; II, pl. 22, Fig. 45.

E. Lambert, "Manet et l'Espagne," *Gazette des Beaux-Arts*, IX (June 1933), p. 379, Fig. 13.

Art News (16 December 1933), p. 11.

R. H. Wilenski, *French Painting* (1936), p. 245.

New York Times Rotogravure Section (14 March 1937).

Art Digest (15 March 1937), p. 9.

A. P. McMahon, "Manet Fifty Years Later," *Parnassus* (March 1937), p. 8.

H. Huth, "Impressionism Comes to America," *Gazette des Beaux-Arts*, XXIX (April 1946), p. 242.

L. Venturi, *Les Archives de l'Impressionisme* (1939) II, p. 190.

A. Tabarant, *Manet et ses Oeuvres* (1947) no. 113, pp. 115-116, 323, 492, 536; repr. p. 605.

M. Florisonne, *Manet* (1947), pp. XIX & XXI.

J. Bouchot-Saupique, "Etudes de quelques dessins de Manet faisant partie de l'ancienne collection Pellerin," *Bulletin de la Société de l'Histoire de l'Art Français* (1960), p. 134.

F. Daulte, "Un siècle d'art français dans les collections suisses à l'Orangerie des Tuileries," *La Revue du Louvre et des Musées de France* (1967), XVII, 3, p. 143.

P. Pool and S. Orienti, *The Complete Paintings of Manet* (1967), no. 97, repr. p. 95.

EXHIBITIONS

London, "Third Exhibition of the Society of French Artists," 1872, no. 31.

Paris, École des Beaux-Arts, "Exposition des oeuvres de Édouard Manet," January 1884, no. 44.

New York, National Academy of Design, "Special Exhibition: Works in Oil and Pastel by the Impressionists of Paris," 1886, no. 240.

Berlin, "Der elften Ausstellung der Berlinner Secession," 1906, no. 189, repr.

Buffalo, Albright Art Gallery, "25th Anniversary of the Opening of the Albright Art Gallery," 16 November-14 December 1930, no. 32, repr.

St. Louis, City Art Museum, "Loan Exhibition of French Painting, 1800-1880," January 1931, no. 17, repr.

Paris, Musée de l'Orangerie, "Exposition Manet," 1932, no. 37, repr.

Philadelphia, Philadelphia Museum of Art, "Manet-Renoir Exhibition," December 1933-January 1934.

San Francisco, California Palace of the Legion of Honor, "Exhibition of French Painting from the XV Century to the Present Day," 8 June-8 July 1934, no. 118.

Boston, Museum of Fine Arts, "Independent Painters of 19th Century Paris," 15 March-28 April 1935, no. 25.

New York, Wildenstein and Co., "Édouard Manet," 19 March-17 April 1937, no. 15, repr. pl. XV.

Toledo, The Toledo Museum of Art, "Paintings by French Impressionists and Post-Impressionists," 7 November-12 December 1937, no. 13, repr.

Amsterdam, Stedelijk Museum, "Honderd Jaar Fransche Kunst," 2 July-25 September 1938, no. 141.

Detroit, Detroit Institute of Arts, "Two Sides of the Medal: French Painting from Gérôme to Gauguin," 1954, no. 20, repr.

Lausanne, Palais de Beaulieu, "Chefs-d'Oeuvres des collections suisses de Manet à Picasso," 1964, no. 350 (not in catalogue; listed in English language guide).

Philadelphia, Philadelphia Museum of Art, "Édouard Manet," 3 November-11 December 1966, no. 76, repr.

Chicago, The Art Institute of Chicago, "Édouard Manet," 13 January-19 February, 1967.

Paris, Musée de l'Orangerie, "Chefs-d'oeuvres des collection suisses de Manet à Picasso," 1967, no. 29, repr. in color.

COLLECTIONS

Durand-Ruel Galleries, Paris (purchased from the artist 1872);
Ernest Hoschedé, Paris (sale, Hôtel Drouot, Paris, 5-6 June, 1878, no. 45);
Fernand Crouan, Nantes;
Rothermundt, Blasewitz;
Paul Cassirer, Berlin;
Joseph Stransky, New York;
Adolphe Lewisohn, New York (by 1928);
Wildenstein and Co., New York (by 1930);
Private Collection, Switzerland;
Wildenstein and Co., New York (by 1968);
The Norton Simon Foundation, Los Angeles (1968).

Edgar Degas

Born 1834 as Hilaire Germain Edgar de Gas in Paris;
died 1917.

Son of a prominent banker, who provided him with an
excellent education in preparation for the study of law.
In 1855, after meeting Ingres, he entered the *École des
Beaux-Arts*, under a pupil of Ingres named Lamothe.
The attitude of Ingres towards classical drawing, and
many Italian Renaissance masters he carefully copied in
Paris and Italy, were his formative influences. He contributed historical subjects and portraits to the *Salon*
between 1865 and 1870, when he served in the war
with his friend Manet. In 1872-1873 he visited New
Orleans. By this time he had left the *Salon*, and started
to modify his style, presumably under the influence of
Manet. Throughout the 1870s his palette lightens, his
line loosens, and his interest focuses on momentary impressions of contemporary life as seen from unusual
viewpoints. An independent spirit, he did not like the
term "Impressionist," but he participated in the first
exhibition of 1874, and organized most of the others.
A gentlemen of broadly cultivated interests, he was devoted to music, opera, ballet and theater; and formed
a collection of work by El Greco, Ingres and Delacroix,
as well as Manet, Renoir, Pissarro, Sisley, Gauguin and
Cézanne. His brilliant mind allowed him to explore
and master numerous media, and subtle combinations
of media, from thinned oil and watercolor to tempera,
etching, drypoint, aquatint, lithograph and monotype.
As his eyes began to fail in the 1880s, he used primarily
pastels. After 1898, when he became almost totally
blind, he was able to devote his last years to the creation
of the only significant sculpture ever generated by a
member of the Impressionistic group.

30. THE BALLET—THREE DANCERS (DANCE LESSON) (ca. 1873)

Oil on canvas, 18-1/4 x 24-1/4 in.
(46 x 61 cm.)

Stamped with mark of *Vente Degas*, lower left:
"Degas"

REFERENCES
P. A. LEMOISNE, *Degas et son oeuvre* (1946), II, no. 332,
p. 170, repr. p. 171.

COLLECTIONS
Atelier Degas, Paris (sale, Galerie Georges Petit, Paris, 3rd
sale of work from Degas' studio, Paris, 7 April 1919,
no. 11, repr.);
Jacques de Zoubaloff, Paris (sale, Galerie Georges Petit, Paris,
17 June 1927, no. 115, repr.);
Diéterle, Paris;
Albert S. Henraux, Paris;
Private Collection, London (sale, Sotheby's, London, 29
March 1964, no. 33);
Ferber and Maison, London (1964);
Paul Rosenberg & Co., New York (by 1969);
The Norton Simon Foundation, Los Angeles (1969).

REMARKS
This painting has been framed to exhibit the dancer on the
right. For an illustration of the entire work see Lemoisne.

31. NURSES ON THE BEACH (ca. 1875)

L'essence on mauve paper mounted on canvas,
17-1/2 x 23-3/4 in. (45.5 x 60.5 cm.)

Stamped with mark of *Vente Degas*, lower left:
"Degas"

REFERENCES

Kunst und Kunstler, XXXII (1933), p. 84 repr.
P. A. LEMOISNE, *Degas et son oeuvre* (1946), II. no. 374,
    p. 200, repr. p. 201.

EXHIBITIONS

Paris, Galerie Paul Rosenberg, "Dessins et pastels de
    Degas," 1932.
Los Angeles, Los Angeles County Museum of Art, "Degas,"
    1958, no. 24, repr. in color.

COLLECTIONS

Atelier Degas (sale, Galerie Georges Petit, Paris, 3rd sale of
    work from Degas' studio, Paris, 7 April 1919, no. 34, repr.);
René Degas, Paris (7 April 1919);
Paul Rosenberg, Paris;
Mrs. A. Chester Beatty, London;
Henri Lerolle, Paris;
Paul Rosenberg and Co., New York (by 1957);
Robert Ellis Simon, Los Angeles (1957);
The Norton Simon Foundation, Los Angeles (1969).

32. THE STAR: DANCER ON POINT (L'ÉTOILE: PREMIER SUJET, DANSEUSE SUR UNE POINTE) (ca. 1877-1878)

Gouache and pastel on paper, 21-1/2 x 29 in.
(56 x 75 cm.)
Signed, lower left: "Degas"

REFERENCES

P. A. LEMOISNE, "La Collection de M. Alexis Rouart," *Les Arts* (March 1908), repr.

P. A. LEMOISNE, *Degas* (1912), repr., p. 65.

The Studio, Vol. 73, p. 1133, repr.

G. MOORE, "Memories of Degas," *Burlington Magazine,* XXXII (January 1918), p. 23, pl. 1.

H. HERTZ, *Degas* (1920), pl. 17, repr.

J. B. MANSON, *The Life and Work of Edgar Degas* (1927), pl. 40, repr. (as L'Étoile).

M. REBATET, *Degas* (1944), pl. 78, repr.

P. A. LEMOISNE, *Degas et son oeuvre* (1946), II, no. 493, p. 272, p. 273 repr.

L. BROWSE, *Degas Dancers* (1949), pl. 54, repr.

J. LEMAYRIE, *L'Impressionism* (1955), II, p. 86, repr.

P. CABANE, *Edgar Degas* (1958), p. 115, pl. 32, repr.

EXHIBITIONS

New York, Wildenstein and Co., "Degas," 7 April to 14 May 1949, no. 44, repr. p. 50 (as *Dancer in White*).

Los Angeles, Los Angeles County Museum, "Degas," 1958, no. 32, repr. p. 43.

COLLECTIONS

Alexis Rouart Sale (4th sale of work from Degas' studio, Paris May 1911, no. 215, repr.);

Galerie Bernheim-Jeune, Paris;

Sir William Eden, Bart., London (sale, Christie's, London, 1 March 1918, no. 104);

Mrs. R. A. Workman, London and United States;

Jakob Goldschmidt, New York and Paris;

Wildenstein and Co., New York;

Grover A. and Jeanne J. Magnin, San Francisco (sale, Parke-Bernet, New York, 15 October 1969, p. 24, no. 6, repr. in color);

The Norton Simon Foundation, Los Angeles (15 October 1969).

33. ACTRESS IN HER DRESSING ROOM
(ca. 1878-1880)

Oil on canvas, 34-1/4 x 28-3/4 in. (83 x 73 cm.)

Signed, upper left: "Degas"

REFERENCES

A. VOLLARD, *Album Degas*, repr., pl. 77.

P. A. LEMOISNE, *Degas et son oeuvre* (1946), II, no. 516,
    p. 286, repr. p. 287.

EXHIBITIONS

London, Lefevre Gallery, "Corot to Cézanne," June 1936,
    no. 18.

COLLECTIONS

Ambroise Vollard, Paris;

Mark Oliver, London (1936);

Alex Reid and Lefevre, Ltd., London (1936);

Mrs. Gilbert Russell, London (1936);

Arthur Tooth and Sons, Ltd., London (by 1964);

Norton Simon, Los Angeles (1964) (sale, Parke-Bernet, New
    York, 5 May 1971, no. 33, repr. in color);

Michael Drinkhouse, New York (1971);

Stephen Hahn Gallery, New York (by 1972);

The Norton Simon Foundation, Los Angeles (1972).

Eugène Boudin

Born 1824 in Honfleur; died 1898

Son of a harbor pilot. In Le Havre as a youth he was employed in a stationery store. Although he had no training and very little means to acquire supplies, he spent much of his time drawing, and was encouraged by visiting artists who displayed works in his shop, especially Troyon and Millet. Having saved some money from the sales of his watercolors, he left for Paris in 1847 where he worked alone, studying Dutch old masters in the Louvre. In 1851, he was awarded a three-year grant by the city of Le Havre. Instead of the academic studio work which was expected, he painted in the open air, and was the first with Daubigny to do so almost exclusively. In 1859, when his work was shown at the *Salon,* Baudelaire and Courbet were impressed, and Corot called him "king of skies." During 1856-1857 Boudin met young Monet in a frame shop where both had works exhibited. Monet (then doing caricatures) was at first critical of the older artist's work, and reluctant to join Boudin in painting out-of-doors. When he did, Monet learned to observe nature directly through all its subtle fluctuations. It was a moment of enlightenment for Monet: "Suddenly a veil was torn away. I had understood—I had realized what painting could be." Appropriately, Boudin was invited to show in the first Impressionist Exhibition of 1874, and spent the rest of his quiet life painting beach and harbor scenes of exquisite sensibility.

34. BEACH AT TROUVILLE. 1873
   Oil on board, 8-1/4 x 16-1/4 in.
   (20.6 x 41.2 cm.)
   Signed, lower left: "E. Boudin"
   Inscribed and dated, lower right: "Trouville 73"

COLLECTIONS
Private Collection, Paris;
M. Knoedler and Co., New York (by 1968);
The Norton Simon Foundation, Los Angeles (1968).

Claude Oscar Monet

Born 1840 in Paris; died 1926.

Son of a grocer who established his family in Le Havre when Claude was five. The sea had a decisive influence on his sensibility. As a youth he was impressed with the luminosity and movement of Corot, Daubigny and Troyon. And he was enriched by the example of Courbet and Manet. But the masters who guided him towards instigating the revolution of Impressionism were Boudin and Jongkind. In 1859 he went to Paris to study, not at the *École* (as his parents wished), but the *Académie Suisse*, where he met Pissarro. After two years of military service in Algeria between 1860 and 1862, he returned to Gleyre's studio where he became friends with Renoir, Bazille and Sisley. Between 1863 and 1866, he led his fellow students in the study of both figures and landscapes in the open air at Fontainebleau. During the next two years this small core of the soon-to-be Impressionist group continued to be rejected by the *Salon*, consider suicide, starve and develop their new style. By 1869, Monet and Renoir while working together had succeeded. It was Monet's idea to hold regular exhibitions of their group, during the first of which, in 1874, their name was derived from the title of one of his paintings. In 1880 he veered away from the group and alone pursued Impressionism to its ultimate extreme. After decades of poverty, his work began to sell. In 1890 he was able to construct the beautiful water garden at Giverny which inspired him for the rest of his life. Unhampered by failing eyes, he accepted Clemenceau's invitation of 1914 to paint murals of his waterlilies which were installed in the Orangerie in 1922. The depth and breadth of his accomplishment is extraordinary. Few painters in the entire history of art have exerted so much influence.

35. ENTRANCE TO THE PORT OF
HONFLEUR (ca. 1868)
Oil on canvas, 19-3/4 x 24 in. (50.5 x 61.2 cm.)
Signed and dedicated, lower left: "A son ami Lafont, 1870, Claude Monet"

REFERENCES
D. WILDENSTEIN, *Monet* (1971), p. 19, no. 3, repr. in color.

EXHIBITIONS
Paris, Galerie des Beaux-Arts, "Monet," 19 June-17 July 1952, no. 16.
The Hague, Gemeentemuseum, "Monet," 24 July-22 September 1952, no. 17.
London, Lefevre Gallery, "Claude Monet, the Early Years," 3 May-7 June 1969, no. 6, repr.

COLLECTIONS
Antoine Lafont, Paris (a gift from the artist);
Private collection, Paris (sale, Hôtel Drouout, Paris, 28 June 1943);
Private collection, Paris;
Galerie Castiglione, Schaan, Liechtenstein (by 1969);
The Norton Simon Foundation, Los Angeles (1969).

REMARKS
Although dated 1870, the picture was probably painted in 1868 and was subsequently dedicated to Lafont two years later. Antoine (or Antonin) Lafont, a journalist, was a witness at Monet's marriage to Camille on 28 June 1870. He later became a deputy for Paris and was a friend of Clemenceau.

Pierre Auguste Renoir

Born 1841 in Limoges; died 1919.

Son of a tailor who brought his family to Paris in 1845. At thirteen, the talented youth was apprenticed to a maker of 18th century style porcelain. From this exposure blossomed his love of Watteau, Boucher and Fragonard whose work he frequently studied in the Louvre. In the early 1860s, at Gleyre's studio, he became friends with Bazille, Pissarro, Sisley, and especially Monet. His early affection for the solidity of Courbet and the vibrant color of Delacroix was guided by Monet into the outdoor painting which, in their hands, developed out of the woods of Fontainebleau into Impressionism. Most of Renoir's supreme masterpieces were painted in the decade between the late 1860s and the early 1880s. After a period of traveling around Europe and North Africa, he was influenced by his appreciation for Raphael, Rubens and Velázquez to alter his approach. From the spontaneity of recording visual stimuli directly, he moved to the more elaborate preparation of careful preliminary drawings. In his Post-Impressionist work, which began in the early 1880s, he composed with color-schemes of reds and pinks that were more abstract than natural. Throughout most of his life Renoir was financially insecure. His fortunes did not start to turn until the Durand-Ruel exhibition of 1892. By the Autumn *Salon* of 1904 he was an international success. In 1906 he moved to the south of France. Crippled by arthritis, his last works were done with brushes stuck between his knuckles or strapped to his wrist. Although his work is the most uneven of all the Impressionists, his mind was always open to ideas as fresh as those of his friend and neighbor, Matisse—the fauve ("wild beast") who was to lead painting into the 20th century.

36. LE PONT DES ARTS, PARIS (ca. 1868)
Oil on canvas, 24-1/2 x 40-1/2 in. (62 x 103 cm.)
Signed, lower right: "A. Renoir"

REFERENCES
J. MEIER-GRAEFE, *Renoir* (1929), pp. 28, 437. repr. p. 29.
J. REWALD, "Paysage de Paris," *La Renaissance* (Jan.-Feb. 1937) repr.
Magazine of Art, XXXII (1939), p. 34, repr.
The Burlington Magazine, LXXIV (1939), p. 40, repr. p. 41.
Magazine of Art, XXXIII (July 1940) p. 407, repr.
J. REWALD, *The History of Impressionism* (1961), pp. 272, 354, and repr. p. 167, in color.
Art News, Vol. 67 (October 1968), pp. 38-39, repr. in color.
M. BRUMER, "Art Boom," *Arts Magazine*, Vol. 43 (1968), p. 9.
T. B. HESS, "Impressionist Patterns in the Art Market," *Art News*, Vol. 67 (January 1969), pp. 27 ff.
W. SEITZ, "The Relevance of Impressionism," *Art News*, Vol. 67 (1969), p. 29.
R. MULLER-MEHLIS, "Warum ist Kunst so Teuer," *Epoca* (April 1970), pp. 60-61, repr. in color.
L. NOCHLIN, *Realism* (1972), repr. p. 220.

EXHIBITIONS
London, Durand-Ruel Galleries, 1872.
New York, Knoedler Galleries, "Views of Paris," 1939, no. 34, repr.
New York, Durand-Ruel Galleries, "Paris," 1940, no. 18.
New York, Wildenstein Galleries, "Renoir," 1950, no. 2, repr.
Detroit, Detroit Institute of Art, "The Two Sides of the Medal," 1954, no. 59, repr.
New York, Wildenstein Galleries, "Renoir," 1958, no. 1, repr.
Washington, D.C., National Gallery of Art, "Masterpieces of Impressionist and Post-Impressionist Paintings," 1959, p. 39, repr.
New York, Wildenstein Galleries, "Olympia's Progeny," 1965, no. 3, repr.
New York, Knoedler Galleries, "Impressionist Treasures," 1966, no. 28, repr.
Philadelphia, Philadelphia Museum of Art, "Recent Acquisitions by the Norton Simon, Inc. Museum of Art," 1969, no. 10 repr. in color.
Chicago, The Art Institute of Chicago, "Renoir Paintings and Drawings," 1973, repr. in color.

COLLECTIONS
Durald-Ruel, Paris (acquired from the artist in 1872);
Comtesse de Rasty, Paris;
Galerie Mattiessen, Berlin (by 1929);
A. Silverberg, Paris (by 1932), (sale, Galerie Georges Petit, Paris, 9 June 1932, no 25, repr.);
Dr. van Kricken;
M. Knoedler and Co., New York (by 1941);
Mrs. W. Clifford Klenk (formerly Mrs. Richard Ryan), (1941-1968), (sale, Parke-Bernet, New York, 9 October 1968, no. 8, repr. in color);
The Norton Simon Foundation, Los Angeles (1968).

37. YOUNG WOMAN IN BLACK (ca. 1876)
Oil on canvas, 12-3/8 x 9-1/4 in.
(31.5 x 23.5 cm.)
Signed upper right: "Renoir"

REFERENCES

TRUBLOT, *La Collection Murer* (1887), no. 39.
P. GACHET, *Deux Amis des Impressionistes, le Docteur Gachet et
Murer* (1956), p. 171.
F. DAULTE, *Auguste Renoir: Catalogue Raisonné de l'oeuvre peint*,
I (1971), no. 165, repr.

EXHIBITIONS

Paris, Grand-Palais, "Salon d'Automne," 15 October-
15 November 1904, no. 5.
Paris, Galerie Bernheim-Jeune, "Renoir Portraitiste,"
10 June-27 July 1938, no. 17.

COLLECTIONS

Eugène Murer, Paris (by 1887);
George Viau, Paris (sale, Galerie Durand-Ruel, Paris,
4 March 1907, no. 66);
Bernheim-Jeune, Paris (4 March 1907)
Paul Harth, Paris;
Etienne Bignou, Paris;
William A. Cargill, Carruth, Scotland (sale, Sotheby & Co.,
London, 11 June 1963, no. 36, repr. in color);
Arthur Tooth and Sons, Ltd. (11 June 1963);
Norton Simon, Los Angeles (1963).

Frédéric Bazille

Born 1841 in Montpellier; died 1870.

Son of a prosperous, well educated vintner, who also was a friend of the distinguished collector, Alfred Bruyas, who owned works by Géricault, Delacroix, Corot, Millet, Diaz and many by Courbet. It is this patron who is commemorated in *Bonjour Monsieur Courbet* (Musée Fabre, Montpellier). From the time that visit took place in 1854, Courbet remained one of Bazille's most important influences. At the University of Montpellier, Bazille studied medicine for three years, and went to Paris to continue in 1862. There he was irresistibly attracted to Gleyre's studio where he became friends with Monet, Renoir and Sisley. Under the strong influence of Monet, whose poverty he frequently relieved, Bazille began to paint figures and landscapes out-of-doors in the direction of Impressionism. But he never lost his desire to give "every subject its weight and volume, and not only paint the appearance." His potential was considerable. The greatest loss to the Impressionist group inflicted by the Franco-Prussian War was the death of Bazille.

38. WOMAN IN MOORISH COSTUME. 1869
Oil on canvas, 35-1/2 x 23-1/2 in. (97 x 58 cm.)
Signed, lower right: "F. Bazille"

REFERENCES
G. POULAIN, *Bazille et ses Amis* (1932), no. 32, repr.
F. DAULTE, *Frédéric Bazille et son temps* (1952) no. 45, p. 184.
F. DAULTE, "Bazille; son oeuvre s'achève en 1870,"
Connaissance des Arts (December 1970), repr. p. 88.

EXHIBITIONS
Paris, Salon d'Automne, "Bazille Retrospective," 1910, no. 18.
Montpellier, Exposition Internationale, "Bazille Retrospective," 1927, no. 30.
Paris, Association des étudiants protestants, "Frederic Bazille," 1935, no. 4.
Montpellier, Musée Fabre, "Centenaire de Bazille," 1941, no. 30.

COLLECTIONS
Family of the artist;
Meynier de Salinelles;
Pinchinat, Nimes (1942);
Private Collection;
E. V. Thaw and Co., Inc., New York (by 1969);
The Norton Simon Foundation, Los Angeles (1969).

Camille Jacob Pissarro

Born 1830 in Saint Thomas, Virgin Islands; died 1903.

Son of a Creole mother and a French father of Por-
tuguese-Jewish descent. After schooling in Paris, he
clerked in his father's general store from 1847 until his
reluctant parents sent him back to Paris in 1855. He was
encouraged by Corot to paint landscape directly rather
than from memory. Pissarro was admitted to the *Salon*
of 1859 and intermittently thereafter. Working out-of-
doors with Monet in the mid 1860s, he developed his
basic attitude towards painting. He was a remarkably
consistent artist and personality. He was the only painter to exhibit in all eight of the Impressionist exhibitions
between 1874 and 1886. As its oldest and most faithful member, he was principally responsible for keeping
the loose group together. Responsive to newly developing ideas, he also contributed to the demise of the Impressionist group by introducing to it Cézanne, Gauguin, Van Gogh, Seurat and Signac. Although not the
most important Impressionist artist, his enormous out-
put attained a high level of quality more often than
some of his fellow painters. Moreover, as a propagand-
ist, conciliator, arbiter, friend, and catalyst of self-
development in more important artists, his contribution to the history of painting is considerable. Almost
all his work was accomplished while he and his family
lived in extreme poverty. Financial success did not come
until the Durand-Ruel retrospective of 1892. By then
his eyesight had started to fail.

39. PONTOISE, BANKS OF THE OISE. 1872
Oil on canvas, 21-1/4 x 28-3/4 in. (54 x 73 cm.)
Signed and dated, lower left: "C. Pissarro. 1872"
Inscribed on back: "A Nunes, 53 rue de
Mauberge"

REFERENCES
L'Art et Les Artistes (February 1918), repr.
T. Duret, *Die Impressionisten* (1918), repr.
L. Pissarro and L. Venturi, *Camille Pissarro* (1939), I,
p. 104, no. 182, repr.

EXHIBITIONS
Paris, Galerie Durand-Ruel, "L'Oeuvre de Camille Pissarro,"
7-30 April 1904, no. 19 (as Vue de Pontoise).
London, Leggatt Brothers, "The Collection of the Rt. Hon.
The Earl of Inchcape," 1961, no. 13, repr.
London, Wildenstein, "The French Impressionists and Some
of Their Contemporaries," 23 April-18 May, 1963, no. 1.
Berkeley, University Art Museum, "Excellence," 1970.

COLLECTIONS
A. Nunes, Paris;
I. Montaignac, Paris (sale, Galerie Georges Petit, Paris,
3-4 December 1917, no. 73);
Mme. B. Halphen, Paris;
Johan Hansen;
Renou et Colle, Paris;
Sam Salz, Paris;
André Weil, Paris;
Wildenstein and Co., New York;
Leggatt Brothers, London;
Earl of Inchcape, London;
Lock Galleries, New York (by 1968);
The Norton Simon Foundation, Los Angeles (1968).

Alfred Sisley

Born 1839 in Paris; died 1899.

Son of a successful English silk merchant living in Paris. At eighteen he was sent to London to learn English, and follow in his father's footsteps. However, he spent most of his time in museums studying Turner and Constable. In 1862 he entered Gleyre's studio where he became friends with Monet, Renoir and Bazille with whom he painted in the woods of Fontainebleau under the very strong influence of Corot and Daubigny. He began exhibiting at the *Salons* of 1866, 1868, and 1870; then at the Impressionist exhibitions of 1874, 1876, 1877 and 1882. He was the most limited of the major Impressionist painters. He was the only one to restrict his subject-matter exclusively to landscape, and the only one who never made any significant developments in his style after the 1870s. Without the financial support of his father, whose business collapsed during the Franco-Prussian War, Sisley was forced to earn his living as an artist. His delicate landscapes, including Impressionism's best scenes of winter, never really sold. He was reduced to painting fans.

40. LOUVECIENNES IN THE SNOW. 1872
Oil on canvas, 20 x 29 in. (51 x 74 cm.)
Signed and dated, lower left: "Sisley '72"

REFERENCES
F. DAULTE, *Alfred Sisley: Catalogue Raisonné* (1959), no. 52, repr.

EXHIBITIONS
Paris, Galerie Georges Petit, "A. Sisley," February 1897, no. 142.
Paris, Galerie Georges Petit, "Alfred Sisley," 14 May-7 June 1917, no. 30.
London, Arthur Tooth and Sons, "Paris-Londres," 1951, no. 4, repr.
London, Tate Gallery, "The Pleydell-Bouverie Collection," 26 January-25 April 1954, no. 33, repr.
Berkeley, University Art Museum, "Excellence," 1970.

COLLECTIONS
Picq-Veron, Paris, (sale, Durand-Ruel, Paris, 25 June 1892);
H. Vever, Paris (17 July 1892), (sale, Galerie George Petit, Paris, 1-2 February 1897, no. 112);
Mme. Cancurte, Paris;
Arthur Tooth and Sons, Ltd., London (by 1951);
Mrs. Audrey E. Pleydell-Bouverie, London (by 1954);
David Gibbs, New York (by 1968);
The Norton Simon Foundation, Los Angeles (1968).

Stanislas Lépine

Born 1835 in Caen; died 1892

A pupil of Corot, Lépine was also influenced by Johan Jongkind (1819-1891) whom he greatly admired. His work was first exhibited in the *Salon* of 1859, but it was not until he won the attention of Count Doria that Lépine's professional status became secure. Under the patronship of the Count, Lépine was relieved of material problems and was free to develop his own style of painting. His favorite subjects were the bridges and barges of the Seine which he painted with delicacy and freshness. By the 1870s, his reputation as an artist was well established, and he was included in the first Impressionist exhibition of 1874.

41. LE PONT-NEUF, PARIS (ca. 1880)
   Oil on canvas, 9 x 13 in. (23 x 33 cm.)
   Signed, lower left: "S. Lepine"

EXHIBITIONS
Paris, Galerie Schmit, "Lépine" (15 May-15 June 1968), no. 59, repr.

COLLECTIONS
Allard and Noel, Paris;
Galerie Schmit, Paris (by 1968);
The Norton Simon Foundation, Los Angeles (1969).

Mary Cassatt

Born 1844 in Pittsburgh; died 1926

Daughter of a wealthy banker, she became identified with French Impressionism both as a painter and as a sponsor of Impressionist works among major American collectors. After having completed four years of study at the Pennsylvania Academy of Arts in Philadelphia, she left for Europe where she travelled extensively, studying and copying works of the old masters in European museums. She settled in Paris in 1874 to study with an academic painter named Chaplin, but soon came to know and admire the work of Courbet, Manet, Monet and especially Degas in 1877. Having been accepted for several years in the *Salon* exhibitions, she was asked by Degas to join the Impressionists in their exhibition of 1879. She continued to do so in all but one of their succeeding exhibitions. With Degas and all of the Impressionists, she discovered the art of the Japanese print, the influence of which extended not only to her work as a painter but also as a print-maker—a pursuit in which she was particularly gifted. Among the several Americans who were guided by Miss Cassatt in the acquisition of paintings was Mrs. H. O. Havermeyer of New York whose distinguished collection is now owned by the Metropolitan Museum of Art. On her own she painted women and children almost exclusively, doing so with a sensitivity and charm that gives her a unique position among the artists of her era. From 1912 until her death, she was afflicted with failing eyesight which brought an end to her career.

42. WOMAN READING (LYDIA CASSATT) (1878)

Oil on canvas, 32 x 25-1/2 in. (81 x 64.6 cm.)
Signed, lower left: "Mary Cassatt"

REFERENCES
A. BREESKIN, Mary Cassatt: *A Catalogue Raisonné of the Oils, Pastels, Watercolors and Drawings* (1970), no. 52, repr.

EXHIBITIONS
Omaha, Joslyn Art Museum, "Mary Cassatt Among the Impressionists," 10 April-1 June, 1969, no. 10, repr. in color.

COLLECTIONS
Durand-Ruel, Paris;
Sam Salz, Inc., New York;
Clare Booth Luce, New York;
Galerie des Arts Anciens et Modernes, Liechtenstein (by 1968);
The Norton Simon Foundation, Los Angeles (1968).

REMARKS
The sitter for this painting has been identified as Lydia Cassatt, the artist's sister. An oil sketch of this painting is in the Joslyn Art Museum, Omaha, Nebraska. Breeskin dates both canvases 1878.

Paul Cézanne

Born 1839 in Aix-en-Provence; died 1906.

Son of a successful local banker, who sent him to the University of Aix and seriously objected to his desire to paint rather rather than practice law. Cézanne's resolve was encouraged by his childhood friend, Émile Zola. Moving to Paris for the first time in 1861, he responded to the robust qualities of the 16th century Venetians, the 17th century Spaniards, as well as Rubens, Delacroix and Daumier. Among his contemporaries, Courbet and Manet were influential in his melodramatic work of the 1860s, and his gentle friend Pissarro in the landscapes of the 1870s, when he reluctantly exhibited with the Impressionist group in 1874 and 1877. Their style was aimed at capturing experiences that were too transitory for him. He wanted "to make of impressionism something solid and enduring like the art of the museums. . . . I wanted to make Poussin over again after nature." Uncomfortable in café discussions of theory, and deeply hurt by the rejection of critics and the *Salon*, he inherited his father's fortune in 1886, and withdrew to the family house in Jas-de-Bouffan, near Aix. There he pitted himself against the heroic odds of a timid outcast with a violent temperament, and lack of natural skill. Slowly and painfully, he proceeded to create a body of work which fundamentally altered the history of art, and has acted as one of the primary influences on the development of painting and sculpture from Cubism to the Minimal Art of today. Recognition began as he was invited to the Brussels show of Les XX in 1890, and the Vollard exhibition of 1895. By the turn of the century, his universal genius was being publically appreciated.

43. VASE OF FLOWERS (ca. 1879-1882)
Oil on canvas, 18-1/2 x 21-3/4 in. (40 x 50 cm.)

REFERENCES

L. VENTURI, *Cézanne, son art-son oeuvre*, (1936), Vol. I, no. 358, p. 143, repr. Vol. II, pl. 98.
S. ORIENTI and A. GATTO, *L'Opera completa di Cézanne* (1970), no. 487, repr. p. 109.

EXHIBITIONS

Cologne, "International Exhibitions of Paintings," May-September 1912, no. 132.
Berkeley, University Art Museum, "Excellence," 1970.

COLLECTIONS

A. Vollard, Paris (from the artist);
A. Bonger, Amsterdam (about 1910 on advice of Odilon Redon);
Bonger family until 1966;
Paul Rosenberg & Co., New York (1966-1967);
The Norton Simon Foundation, Los Angeles (1967).

44. FARM HOUSE AND CHESTNUT TREES
AT JAS DE BOUFFAN (ca. 1885)

Oil on canvas, 36 x 29 in. (92 x 73 cm.)

REFERENCES

J. REWALD, *Paul Cézanne, A Biography* (1948), repr. pl. 60.
J. REWALD, *Cézanne and Zola* (1948).
Life (25 February 1952), p. 83, repr. in color.

COLLECTIONS

Given by Cézanne to one of his housekeepers, in whose
    possession it remained for many years;
Paul Rosenberg & Co., New York (by 1957);
Robert Ellis Simon, Los Angeles (1957);
The Norton Simon Foundation, Los Angeles (1969).

Vincent van Gogh

Born 1853 at Groot-Zundert in the Netherlands; died 1890

Son of a Protestant clergyman, Vincent was strongly influenced by the values of his strict Calvinist background. At sixteen he followed the professional example of his uncles and his brother Theo by joining the staff of the Goupil Gallery in The Hague and London. Temperamentally unsuited to be a dealer and emotionally unstable, he was discharged in 1876. Dissatisfied with several other attempts at occupations in bookstores and schools, he decided to study religion in Amsterdam, but was not admitted to the university. His last determined effort to contribute to the well-being of the world was as a lay missionary in the impoverished mining district of Borinage in Belgium. From this position he also was dismissed in 1880, but not before he had begun to sketch the faces of the poor and awaken in himself the possibility of becoming an artist. During the early 1880s he lived primarily with his parents at Nuenen, where he taught himself to draw and paint under the influence of Rembrandt, Rubens, Daumier and Millet. This period of dark sombre canvases ended abruptly when he went to live with Theo in Paris early in 1886. Exhilarated by discovering the light colors and vibrant brushstrokes of Pissarro, Degas, Gauguin, Seurat, Lautrec as well as Japanese prints, he executed over two hundred paintings in twenty months. In 1888 he moved to the sun-drenched fields of Provence at Arles, where he worked at an even more feverish pace. Here he was able to achieve the maturity of his inflamed genius. He worked in desperation against the fear of oncoming madness and the hovering image of death. In late 1888, the anguish of his instability was such that he attacked Gauguin and cut off his own ear. In 1889 he spent many months in the asylum of Saint Rémy, where, between attacks, he was able to paint with complete lucidity and absolute control. In May of 1890 he left Saint Rémy for Auvers, near Paris. There, two months later, he shot himself in the heart. Although his brother was only able to sell a single canvas during Vincent's lifetime, his work has come to mean more to a greater number of people than any painter since Rembrandt. Vincent probably painted more masterpieces in a shorter period of time than any other artist in history. His achievement is so brilliant, it is as if he was able to harmonize the motions of his mind with wavelengths passing through him from the deepest corners of the universe, as if his brushstrokes were dancing on the tip of a cosmic nerve ending.

45. WINTER (1885)

Oil on canvas, mounted on panel,
23-1/4 x 30-3/4 in. (59 x 78 cm.)

REFERENCES

J. DE LA FAILLE, *L'Oeuvre de Vincent van Gogh, Catalogue Raisonné* (1928), I, no. 194; II, no. 194, repr.
J. DE LA FAILLE, *Vincent van Gogh* (1939), no. 209, repr.
W. WILSON, "Two van Goghs for the Price of One," *Calendar* (Los Angeles Times), 4 January 1970, p. 44, repr.
J. DE LA FAILLE, *The Works of Vincent van Gogh, His Paintings and Drawings* (1970), no. F194 [H, 209], repr. p. 145 in color.
J. HULSKER, *"Dagboek" van Van Gogh* (1970), p. 69, repr. in color.

EXHIBITIONS

Amsterdam, Stedelijk Museum, July-August 1905, no. 27.
London, Reid and Lefevre Gallery, "XIX and XX Centruy French Paintings and Drawings," November-December 1966, no. 15.

COLLECTIONS

C. Mouwen, Jr., Breda;
H. P. Bremmer, The Hague (sale, Frederick Muller et Cie, 3 May 1904, no. 6, repr.);
E. J. van Wisselingh and Co., Amsterdam (by 1969);
The Norton Simon Foundation, Los Angeles (1969).

46. THE MULBERRY TREE (1889)
Oil on canvas, 21-1/4 x 25-5/8 in. (54 x 65 cm.)

REFERENCES

Further Letters of Vincent van Gogh to his Brother, 1886-1889
(1929) Letter 609, p. 380; letter 618, p. 400.
W. SCHERJON and J. DE GRUYTER, *Vincent van Gogh's Great
Period, Arles, St. Remy, and Auvers sur Oise,* (1937), p. 247,
no. 53.
J. DE LA FAILLE, *Vincent van Gogh* (1939), p. 441, pl. 640
and F. 627.
J. DE LA FAILLE, *The Works of Vincent van Gogh, His Paintings and
Drawings* (1970), no. F. 637 [H. 640], repr.

EXHIBITIONS

Zurich, Zürcher Kunsthaus, "Franzosische Kunst des XIX und
XX Jahrhunderts," 5 October-4 November 1917, no. 570.
Paris, Bernheim Jeune, "Van Gogh, l'époque Française,"
20 June-2 July, 1927.

COLLECTIONS

Alphonse Kann, Saint-Germain-en-Laye;
Ambroise Vollard, Paris;
Mme. C. Pissarro, Paris;
Marlborough Fine Art, Ltd., London (by 1961);
Norton Simon, Los Angeles (1961).

Paul Gauguin

Born 1848 in Paris; died 1903

Son of a journalist and a Spanish-Peruvian mother from Lima, where he spent four years of his childhood. Continuously attracted by exotic places, he joined the Merchant Marine at seventeen, sailing to Rio de Janeiro and Bahia until he was twenty-one. In 1871 he began his successful career with the brokerage firm of Bertin in Paris, married a Danish woman, and started a family. While enjoying the bourgeois role he would later renounce, he collected works by Manet, Monet, Renoir, Sisley, Pissarro and Cézanne; and admired the linear tradition from Ingres to Degas (who later collected Gauguin's work). He also became a "Sunday" painter, and even had a landscape accepted by the *Salon* of 1876. Inspired by his friend Pissarro, he began to paint more seriously, and exhibited in all the Impressionists' shows from 1880 to 1886. In 1883 he left his job and soon separated from his family. Between 1886 and 1891 Gauguin lived and worked mostly in Brittany in a barefoot and boisterous community of fellow artists at Pont-Aven and Le Pouldu; except for a trip to Martinique and Panama in 1887, and two disastrous months in Arles with Van Gogh in 1888. By then his art was reaching its full maturity in many media, including wood sculpture, ceramics and graphics—work which he used to self-consciously "liberate" a generation of artists from Bernard and Sérrusier to Denis, Bonnard, Vuillard and Maillol. His problem was no longer how to paint, but how to live. This dark, cold, windy north was not a place in which he felt the human spirit could flourish. Believing that he had to free himself from "civilization" he wanted to move his "community" to the tropics. Forced to go alone, he arranged a successful auction of his work, and after being toasted by the symbolist poets of Paris, left for Tahiti in 1891. At first he was very happy there, painted naked in the sun, among people of spiritual purity. Plagued by a lack of money, he had to return to Paris in 1893. After receiving his first one-man show from Durand-Ruel, he returned to the islands in 1895. Living in abject poverty and suffering an excruciating series of illnesses, he did not find what he, and the rest of humanity, are searching for. But he left the 20th century some profoundly beautiful clues.

47. TAHITIAN WOMAN AND BOY. 1899
Oil on canvas, 36-1/2 x 23 in. (95 x 61 cm.)
Signed and dated, lower right:
"99 / Paul Gauguin"

REFERENCES

J. MEIER-GRAEFE, *Entwicklungs-Geschichte der Modernen Kunst*, III (1904), p. 141, repr.
J. DE ROTONCHAMP, *Paul Gauguin, 1848-1903* (1925), p. 221, no. 7.
G. WILDENSTEIN, *Gauguin* (1964), no. 578, repr.

EXHIBITIONS

Manchester, Thos. Agnew and Sons, "Loan Exhibition of Masterpieces of French Art of the 19th Century, in Aid of the Lord Mayor's Appeal for the Hospitals," 1923, no. 18.
New York, Hammer Gallery, "40th Anniversary Loan Exhibition," 7 November-7 December 1968, p. 31, repr. in color in reverse.

COLLECTIONS

Ambroise Vollard, Paris;
Moll, Vienna;
Mrs. Austin Mardon, Andross Castle, Scotland (1923);
Mrs. Austin Mardon (sale, Sotheby & Co., London, 24-25 November, 1964, no. 32, repr. in color);
Hammer Galleries, New York (November 1964);
Norton Simon, Los Angeles (1965).

Henri Raymond de Toulouse-Lautrec

Born 1864 in Albi; died 1901.

Descended from an ancient family of aristocrats who also were amateur artists. His family always provided him with money, but not a great deal more. As a child he was precociously skillful at drawing portraits and horses, which he continued to pursue despite the deformation of abnormally short arms and legs that resulted from breaking his weak bones during adolescence in a riding accident. In 1882-1883 he studied in the academic studios of Bonnat and Cormon, where his chief benefit was meeting Émile Bernard and Van Gogh. After meeting Pissarro, Gauguin, Seurat and Degas, his palette lightened under the impact of Impressionism. The principal influences seem to have been Degas and Japanese prints which Lautrec synthesized into a mature style in the late 1880s. At that time he moved to Montmarte to feast on the night life that centered around music halls and brothels. There, for his one spectacularly productive decade, he was as close as he could be to being at ease. Welcome in a world of the unusual, he delineated a wide ranging life-style with acute humanity. He energized into flaming colored lines the enormous vitality he saw reverberating from all the dancing laughter. And around the sight of sadness, he placed a cloak of special dignity woven from his unique sympathy for suffering. For all his tireless effort, he found it difficult to compensate himself for the pain of being alive. He died a defeated alcoholic.

48. PROFILE OF A PROSTITUTE (1893)

Oil on cardboard, 24-1/4 x 19 in.
(63.3 x 48.5 cm.)
Signed, lower right: "H T Lautrec"

REFERENCES

M. JOYANT, *Henri de Toulouse-Lautrec* (1926), I, p. 284, as "Femme de Maison," repr. p. 199.
J. LASSAIGNE, *Toulouse-Lautrec* (1939), p. 127, as "The Inmate of a Brothel."
G. M. SUGANA and G. CAPRONI, *L'opera completa di Toulouse-Lautrec* (1969), no. 350, p. 109, repr. p. 108.
M. G. DORTU, *Toulouse-Lautrec et son oeuvre* (1971), II, p. 313, no. P509, repr. p. 313.

EXHIBITIONS

Paris, Galerie Paul Rosenberg, 1914, no. 24.
Paris, Galerie Manzi-Joyant, "Toulouse-Lautrec Retrospective," 1914, no. 77.
Paris, Musée des Arts Décoratifs, "Toulouse-Lautrec Trentenaire," 1931, no. 106.
New York, Paul Rosenberg & Co., "French Paintings of the 19th and 20th Centuries," 1945, no. 9.
New York, Paul Rosenberg & Co., "Great French Masters of the 19th Century," 1947, no. 13.
Detroit, Detroit Institute of Arts, "The Two Sides of the Medal," 1954, no. 128 (as "Profil").
Philadelphia, Philadelphia Museum of Art, "Toulouse-Lautrec", 1955, no. 52, repr.
Chicago, The Art Institute of Chicago, "Toulouse-Lautrec," 1956, no. 52, repr.
New York, The Museum of Modern Art, "Toulouse-Lautrec," 1956, no. 24.
Los Angeles, Jewish Women's Council Exhibit, 1959.

COLLECTIONS

Sevadjian (sale, Paris, 22 March 1920, no. 21, repr.);
M. Heibel (by 1920);
Mlle. Jean Renouard, Paris;
Paul Rosenberg & Co., New York (by 1957);
Robert Ellis Simon, Los Angeles (1957);
The Norton Simon Foundation, Los Angeles (1969).

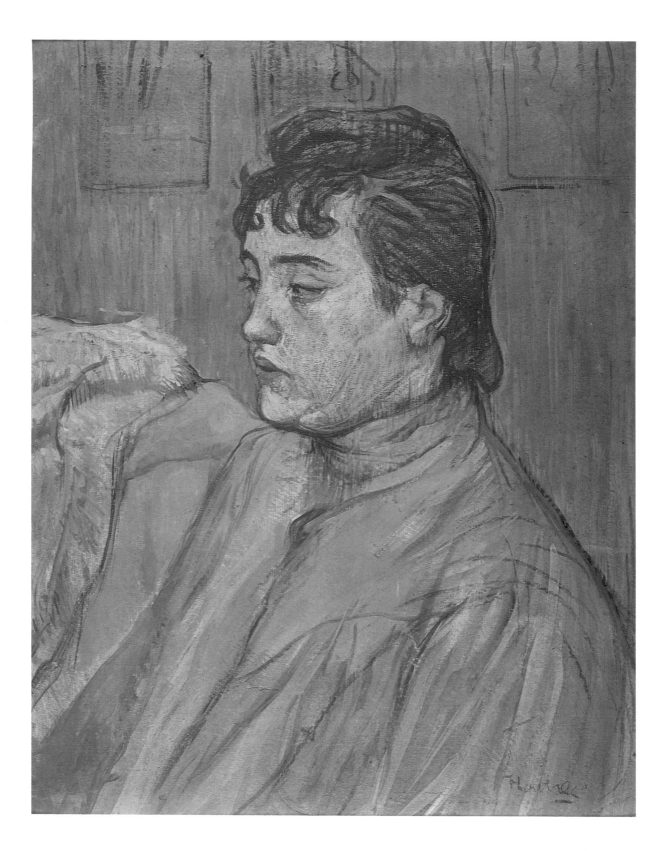

Henri Rousseau

Born 1844 in Laval; died 1910

Son of a tinsmith. Studied law, and between 1864 and 1868 seems to have served as a member of the French Army's regimental band in Mexico, the experience of which filled him with memories of exotic landscape settings. In the Franco-Prussian War he was a sergeant. For the next twenty-two years his vocation was that of a minor customs inspector at the city limits of Paris (hence the nickname "le Douanier"). Among his many avocations were teaching music, writing plays and painting, in which he had no formal instruction other than a word of advice from Gérôme. About 1880 he started to paint and copy in the Louvre, part-time. He retired to devote himself to painting full-time about 1885, and started to exhibit regularly at the *Salon des Indépendents* in 1886. Although he started painting late in life, he had as much "training" and experience as other of his contemporaries, such as Gauguin. Although his technical gifts were not great, it would be inaccurate to describe him as a "Sunday painter," or even naive, except in the most sophisticated sense. He was one of the important Post Impressionists who had the pain and privilege of being self-taught. His work was noticed by Gauguin and Pissarro. After about 1906 he was admired by the literary circle of Guillaume Apollinaire, as well as the Fauves, and Picasso who held a famous banquet for him in 1908.

49. EXOTIC LANDSCAPE. 1910

Oil on canvas, 51-1/4 x 64 in. (130 x 163 cm.)
Signed and dated, lower right: "Henri Rousseau 1910"

REFERENCES

H. KOLLE, *Henri Rousseau* (1922), no. 55, repr.
D. C. RICH, *Henri Rousseau* (1942), repr. p. 72.
J. BOURET, *Henri Rousseau* (1961), p. 157, pl. 49, repr. in color.
D. VALLIER, *Henri Rousseau* (1962) pl. 171, repr.
D. VALLIER, *Rousseau, il Doganiere* (1969), no. 252, pl. 112, Pl. LVIII in color.

EXHIBITIONS

New York, Museum of Modern Art, "Henri Rousseau," 1942.
Chicago, The Art Institute of Chicago, "Henri Rousseau," 1942.
New Haven, Yale University Art Gallery, "Paintings, Drawings and Sculpture Collected by Yale Alumni," 1960, no. 83.
Paris, Galerie Charpentier, "Henri Rousseau dit Le Douanier," Paris, 1961, no. 78, repr.
New York, Wildenstein and Co., "Henri Rousseau," 1963, no. 61, repr.

COLLECTIONS

Tetzen-Lund, Copenhagen (by 1922);
Paul Rosenberg, Paris;
Chester Johnson Galleries, Chicago;
Mrs. Robert R. McCormick, Chicago and Washington (sale, Parke-Bernet, New York, 21 October 1971, no. 90, repr. in color p. 41);
The Norton Simon Foundation, Los Angeles (21 October 1971).

Pierre Bonnard

Born 1867 in Fontenay-aux-Roses; died 1947

Son of an important official in the War Ministry who encouraged him to study law. Bonnard failed to pass the examination for a bureaucratic appointment, as he was spending most of his time painting towards a lyrical synthesis of inspirations from Degas and Monet at the *Académie Julian*. There he met other young painters who were to join together in a group called the "Nabis" (the Hebrew word for prophets or *illuminati*). Members of the group included Paul Sérusier (1863-1927), Maurice Denis (1870-1943), and Édouard Vuillard (1868-1940) who would remain Bonnard's life-time friend. Sérusier visited the "community" of Pont-Aven in 1888. He brought back to his young friends Gauguin's ideas on the symbolic use of color and strong, "primitive" formal patterns, as well as a landscape painted under Gauguin's guidance which became the *Talisman* of their group. The New Art of the Nabis also expressed itself in a vocabulary of symbolic colors and formal relationships, but with less literary subject-matter and greater intimacy. Throughout the 1890s Bonnard's rapidly maturing art flourished not only as a painter, but also as a printmaker, poster and furniture designer. Under the influence of Lautrec (with whom he collaborated), Bonnard's posters and book illustrations are among the finest produced during that decade, which was one of the most brilliant in the history of graphic design. His first one-man show was held at the Durand-Ruel Gallery in 1896. About 1920 he left Paris to divide his time between a village on the Seine, and the shore of the Mediterranean near Cannes. There this gentle, deeply meditative spirit married his lifelong companion, Maria Boursin; and spent the rest of his quiet life, letting his eye follow the flow of sunlight on every flower, fruit, face and figure that it touched.

50. LA PLACE CLICHY, PARIS. 1900
   Oil on cardboard (triptych)
   Left: 13-3/4 x 9-1/2 in. (35 x 24 cm.)
   Center: 13-3/8 x 20-3/4 in. (34 x 53 cm.)
   Right: 13-5/8 x 8-7/8 in. (34.5 x 22.5 cm.)
   Left panel signed, lower left: "Bonnard"
   Center panel signed, and dated, lower left: "1900 Bonnard"
   Right panel signed, lower right: "Bonnard"

REFERENCES

J. and H. DAUBERVILLE, *Bonnard: Catalogue raisonné de l'oeuvre peint, 1888-1905* (1965) p. 241, no. 237, repr.

COLLECTIONS

Joseph Hessel, Paris;
Private Collection, France;
Hirschl and Adler Galleries, Inc., New York (by 1969);
The Norton Simon Foundation, Los Angeles (1969).

Auguste Rodin

Born 1840 in Paris; died 1917

His parents, although poor, wished to provide their son with a suitable education. When he was twelve they were able to enroll him in the boarding school his uncle operated in Beauvais. From 1854 to 1859 he attended *La Petite École,* which emphasized 18th century decorative design. His three attempts to be admitted to the *École des Beaux-Arts* were unsuccessful. During the early 1860s, the death of his sister affected him so deeply he spent a year in a monastery. By 1864 he had decided to become a sculptor; met Rose Beuret who would be his life-long companion; and begun his long apprenticeship as a mason in a studio producing decorative elements for commercial purposes. Later he studied briefly with Barye (1796-1875), but his most important teachers were the Old Masters, especially Michelangelo and Donatello. In 1871 he went to Brussels where he collaborated with Carrier-Belleuse on architectural elements for the new Stock Exchange building. After the inspiration of an Italian visit, he created his first major work, *The Age of Bronze,* in 1876. Because of its life-like appearance Rodin was accused of casting the sculpture from life. His next work, *The Walking Man,* removed itself from the possibility of any such criticism. It began as a study for *St. John the Baptist Preaching* of 1878. But Rodin recognized it as a complete aesthetic entity, fully expressive of his belief that "the human body is a temple that marches." This revolutionary, headless and armless sculpture was Rodin's first exploration of the partial figure, the concept of which led directly to 20th century abstractions.

51. THE WALKING MAN (ca. 1875-1900)
Bronze, 87-7/8 x 29-1/2 x 53-1/8 in.
(223.3 x 74.9 x 135 cm.)
(Edition of 12, cast no. 7)
Signed on top of base between legs: "A. Rodin"
Copyrighted on rear of base: "© Musée Rodin, 1963"
Stamped on left of base: "Georges Rudier, Paris"

REFERENCES
A. ELSEN, *Rodin* (1963), pp. 27-33.
A. ELSEN and H. MOORE, "Rodin's 'Walking Man' as seen by Henry Moore," *Studio International* (July-August 1967), pp. 26-30.
I. JIANOU and C. GOLDSCHEIDER, *Rodin* (1969), p. 86.

EXHIBITIONS
Los Angeles, Los Angeles County Museum of Art, "Sculpture from the Collections of Norton Simon, Inc. and the Hunt Industries Museum of Art," 1968-1969.

COLLECTIONS
Musée Rodin (1963);
Pierre Matisse Gallery, New York (by 1966);
Norton Simon, Inc. Museum of Art, Los Angeles (1966).

REMARKS
The torso of about 1875-1877 was not joined with its legs until about 1900 when the sculpture was first exhibited. The first over life-size cast was executed in 1905 and exhibited in 1907.

147

By the early 1880s Rodin's work was being exhibited frequently, and many public and private commissions were being awarded to him. The one that was to occupy him for the rest of his life was for a portal at the *Musée des Arts Décoratifs* in Paris. The form of *The Gates of Hell* had its point of departure in the Baptistry doors of Ghiberti in Florence. The theme was derived from Dante's *Divine Comedy*. Although never completed, the extraordinary concept of these great doors included in its design many of the most famous works which Rodin later produced individually, such as *the Thinker, Adam, Eve,* and *The Three Shades*. Of the other major commissions, the two most important were *The Burghers of Calais* and *The Monument to Balzac*. The first was commissioned by the city of Calais in 1884, and finally installed there in 1895. As Albert E. Elsen has noted: "*Rodin was undertaking one of the last great works of public sculpture inspired by a specific historical event. He was to re-create from the late-medieval Chronicles of Froissart the heroic sacrifice of the six leading citizens of Calais who, in 1347, during the Hundred Years' War, had donned sackcloth and rope halters to give themselves to King Edward III of England as hostages in return for a lifting of the bloody eleven-months' siege of their city. . . . The commission had many exciting elements for Rodin. He believed, like Delacroix, that art could rival literature as well as be inspired by it, and that the subject should be important and well known. Here he had a great story of moral sacrifice vividly told—one which provided him with latitude for his own imagination. The episode had taken place in medieval France, the period that the artist loved the best and knew the most profoundly. This was to be an occasion for him to treat a theme both medieval and timeless, in a style that he deeply believed was compatible with Gothic art, yet right for his own day. Finally, his work was to be exhibited in an important public place and would contribute to a sense of identity between the community of the living and the dead. Encountered daily, it could serve as a modern equivalent of the religious art of the past which by joining art and life had inspired reverence and exalted feelings.*"

52. THE BURGHERS OF CALAIS (1884-1895)
   Bronze, 82-1/2 x 94 x 75 in.
      (209.5 x 238.8 x 190.5 cm.)
   (Edition of 12, cast no. 10)
   Signed on top of base: "A. Rodin"
   Copyrighted on side of base: " © Musée Rodin, 1969"
   Stamped on rear of base: "Georges Rudier, Fondeur, Paris"

REFERENCES

A. ELSEN, *Rodin* (1963), pp. 70-87.
I. JIANOU, and C. GOLDSCHEIDER, *Rodin* (1969), p. 97.

COLLECTIONS

Musée Rodin, Paris (1969);
Norton Simon, Inc. Museum of Art, Los Angeles (1969).

Rodin's *Monument to Balzac* was commissioned in 1891. He made elaborate efforts to reconstruct the personality of the great novelist who had died in 1850, making use of not only all the available portraits, photographs and literature, but also measurements from the writer's old tailor, and figure studies from similarly structured natives from the countryside of Tours. This was only preparation, of course. The problem was to give expression to what Rodin felt to be inside the man. Although the final figure was not cast until after Rodin's death, it was completed in 1898. The degree to which he succeeded can be measured in his own terms. He called *Balzac* "the sum of my whole life, result of a whole lifetime of effort, the mainspring of my aesthetic theory. From the day of its conception, I was a changed man." *Balzac* opened the world to an understanding of what lies beyond the simple replication of obvious realities; what strength formal values have in their own right; and what power the human form can be invested with when surrounded by a symbol of itself. Rodin is singularly responsible for altering the importance of sculpture in modern consciousness. After the 17th century, sculpture slowly slipped into a position of being a secondary art form. The general public has forgotten almost all the names of those distinguished sculptors who worked between Bernini and Rodin. Because of the new vitality and direction Rodin began, sculpture has become a major art form once again in the 20th century. It is a fitting tribute to his historical importance that the world-wide fame of Rodin today is second only to that of Michelangelo. Throughout the history of humanity, love has not often been able to conquer hate, even for a moment. But when Rodin died, during the middle of the First World War, it was not only France who grieved publicly, and was grateful privately that this great human being had been alive and shared his spirit with them. America, England and even Germany paused, for a moment.

53. MONUMENT TO BALZAC (1891-1898)
Bronze, 117 x 47-1/4 x 47-1/4 in.
  (297.2 x 120 x 120 cm.)
(Edition of 12, cast no. 8)
Signed on base at top right: "A. Rodin"
Stamped on rear of base: "Georges Rudier, Fondeur, Paris"

REFERENCES
A. ELSEN, *Rodin* (1963), pp. 89-105.
J. DE CASO, "Rodin and the Cult of Balzac,"
  Burlington Magazine (June 1964), pp. 278-284.
I. JIANOU and C. GOLDSCHEIDER, *Rodin* (1969), p. 104.

EXHIBITIONS
Los Angeles, Los Angeles County Museum of Art,
  "Sculpture from the Collection of Norton Simon, Inc.
  and the Hunt Industries of Art," August 1968.

COLLECTIONS
Musée Rodin, Paris (1967);
Norton Simon, Inc. Museum of Art, Los Angeles (1967).

Aristide Maillol

Born 1861 in Banyuls; died 1944

From a Catalan family associated with the rural and seafaring life of the southern French seacoast, Maillol grew up in his grandfather's house and was cared for by his devoted aunt. The house was to remain Maillol's home for the rest of his life. After attending college in nearby Perpignan, he went to Paris at the age of twenty, resolved to study art. For the next four years, he studied first with Gérôme at the *École des Arts Décoratifs;* with Cabanel at the *École des Beaux-Arts;* and then left his formal training, dissatisfied with an academic orientation. In the late 1880s Maillol became acquainted with the work of Gauguin and "the Nabi." This exposure led Maillol into the New Art at the end of the century with its strong emphasis on symbolism and spontaneous linearity. His work during these years not only involved painting and sculpture but also ceramic vessels, prints and drawings, and especially the design and production of tapestries. Deeply concerned with the quality of his basic materials, he made his own vegetable dyes in the tapestry workshop, and produced his own paper for graphics. At the beginning of the twentieth century, when his eyes began to weaken, Maillol was inspired by Rodin to find in sculpture his primary mode of expression. Almost exclusively devoted to the female nude, his sculpture emerged from both his roots in the elemental values of the land and sea, and the deep influence of classic Greek art. Reacting to the dramatic contrasts and violent force in Rodin's sculpture, Maillol molded his universal symbols with a quietly vibrant asymmetry and timeless serenity. If the art of Rodin has all the power of a great volcano which erupts only once in several centuries, the art of Maillol is in the current of a great river which is always flowing as it has ever been.

54. DRAPED TORSO (1900)
    Bronze, H: 8-1/4 in. (21 cm.)
    Signed with monogram and numbered on left leg: "AM"; "Epreuve d'artiste"
    Stamped on rear of base: "Alexis Rudier, Fondeur, Paris"

REFERENCES
W. GEORGE, *Aristide Maillol* (1965), repr. p. 182.

COLLECTIONS
Galerie Dina Vierny, Paris (by 1968);
Norton Simon, Inc. Museum of Art, Los Angeles (1968).

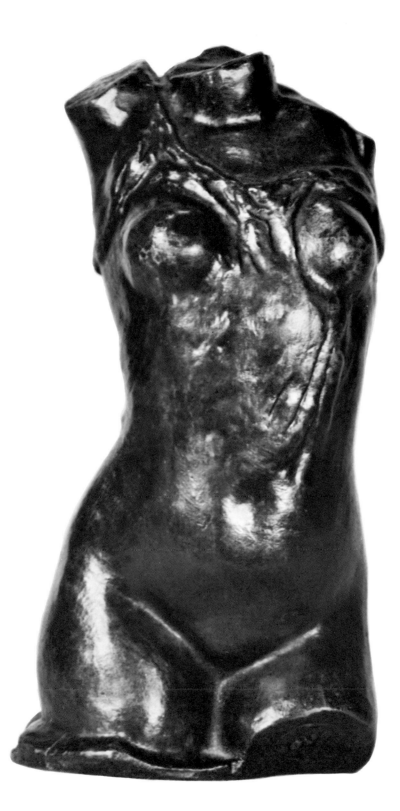

55. CHAINED ACTION (1906)

Bronze, H: 84-5/8 in. (215 cm.)

(Edition of 6, cast no. 5)

Signed with monogram at right of top of base:
"M."

Stamped on rear of base: "Georges Rudier"

REFERENCES

W. GEORGE, *Aristide Maillol* (1965), repr. p. 143.

COLLECTIONS

Estate of the artist;
Galerie Dina Vierny, Paris (by 1970);
Norton Simon, Inc. Museum of Art, Los Angeles (1970).

56. VENUS (1918-1928)

    Bronze, H: 68-1/2 in. (1.75 m.)

    Signed with monogram at rear of base: "AM"

    Stamped on rear of base: "Alexis Rudier,
       Fondeur, Paris".

REFERENCES

RENE-JEAN, *Maillol* (1936), repr.
W. GEORGE, *Maillol* (1971), p. 21, repr. p. 22.

EXHIBITIONS

Paris, Musée National d'Arte Moderne, "Hommage à
    Aristide Maillol," 23 June-2 October 1961, no. 63, p. 32,
    repr. pl. 30.
Los Angeles, Los Angeles County Museum of Art,
    "Sculpture from the Collections of Norton Simon, Inc.
    and the Hunt Industries Museum of Art," 1968-1969.

COLLECTIONS

Galerie Dina Vierny, Paris;
Norton Simon, Inc. Museum of Art, Los Angeles (1962).

57. BATHER WITH A SHOULDER SASH
(1919)

Bronze, H: 13-1/4 in. (34 cm.)

Signed with artist's monogram and marked on right of base: "AM"; "Epreuve d'artiste".

Stamped on rear of base: "Alexis Rudier, Fondeur, Paris".

REFERENCES

W. GEORGE, *Aristide Maillol* (1965), repr. p. 68 in color.

EXHIBITIONS

Paris, Musée National d'Art Moderne, "Hommage à Aristide Maillol" 23 June-2 October 1961, no. 61, repr. pl. 20.

COLLECTIONS

Galerie Dina Viery, Paris;
Norton Simon, Inc. Museum of Art, Los Angeles (1967).

58. WOMAN WITH A THORN (1920)

Bronze, H : 6-7/8 in. (17 cm.)

Signed with artist's monogram and marked on right side of base : "AM"; "Epreuve d'Artiste"

Stamped on rear of base : "Alexis Rudier, Fondeur, Paris".

REFERENCES

W. George, *Aristide Maillol* (1965), repr. p. 175 in color.

COLLECTIONS

Galerie Dina Vierny, Paris;
Norton Simon, Inc. Museum of Art, Los Angeles (1968).

59. WOMAN HOLDING HER FEET (1920)
Bronze, H: 7-1/2 in. (19 cm.)
(Edition of 6, cast no. 4)
Signed on side of base with artist's monogram:
"AM"
Stamped on rear of base: "Alexis Rudier,
Fondeur, Paris".

REFERENCES
W. GEORGE, *Aristide Maillol* (1965), repr. p. 177.

COLLECTIONS
Galerie Dina Vierny, Paris;
Perls Galleries, New York (by 1968);
Norton Simon, Inc. Museum of Art, Los Angeles (1968).

60. WOMAN HOLDING HER FOOT (1920)

Bronze, H: 8 in. (20 cm.)

(Edition of 6, cast no. 6)

Signed on bottom of right foot with the artist's
monogram: "AM"

Stamped on right of base, rear: "Alexis Rudier,
Fondeur, Paris."

REFERENCES

W. George, *Aristide Maillol* (1965), repr. 174 (two views).
W. George, *Maillol* (1971), repr. p. 71.

COLLECTIONS

Galerie Dina Vierny, Paris;
Norton Simon, Inc. Museum of Art, Los Angeles (1967).

61. KNEELING GIRL (1922)

Bronze, H: 39-3/8 in. (100 cm.)

(Edition of 4, cast no. 4)

Signed and numbered on right side of plinth:
"A. Maillol 4/4"

Stamped on base, lower right rear: "Alexis
Rudier, Fondeur, Paris".

EXHIBITIONS

Paris, Musée National de l'Art Moderne, "Hommage à
Aristide Maillol" 23 June-2 October 1961, no. 12.

Irvine, University of California, "A Selection of Nineteenth
and Twentieth Century Works from the Hunt Foods and
Industries Museum of Art," March 1967, repr., p. 32.

Davis, University of California, "A Selection of Nineteenth
and Twentieth Century Works from the Hunt Foods and
Industries Museum of Art," April 1967, repr., p. 32.

Riverside, University of California, "A Selection of Nineteenth
and Twentieth Century Works from the Hunt Foods and
Industries Museum of Art," May 1967, repr., p. 32.

San Diego, University of California, "A Selection of Nineteenth
and Twentieth Century Works from the Hunt Foods and
Industries Museum of Art," July-September 1967, repr.,
p. 32.

COLLECTIONS

Estate of the Artist;
Galerie Dina Vierny, Paris;
Marlborough-Gerson Gallery, Inc., New York (by 1966);
Norton Simon, Inc. Museum of Art, Los Angeles (1966).

167

62. CROUCHED BATHER, HEAD
    LOWERED (1930)

Bronze, 6-1/2 x 4-3/4 in. (17.5 x 21 cm.)

Signed with artist's monogram and marked on
    right side of base: "AM";
    "Epreuve d'Artiste".

Stamped on rear of base: "Alexis Rudier,
    Fondeur, Paris".

REFERENCES

W. GEORGE, *Aristide Maillol* (1965), repr. p. 201 as
    "Crouching Woman."

COLLECTIONS

Galerie Dina Vierny, Paris (by 1967);
Norton Simon, Inc. Museum of Art, Los Angeles (1967).

63. SEATED WOMAN ARRANGING HER
HAIR (1936)

Bronze, H: 9-3/4 in. (24.7 cm.)

(Edition of 6, cast no. 4)

Signed with monogram and numbered on right
side of base: "AM"; "4/6"

Stamped on rear of base: "Alexis Rudier,
Fondeur, Paris".

COLLECTIONS

Estate of the Artist;
Galerie Dina Vierny, Paris;
Perls Galleries, New York (by 1968);
Norton Simon, Inc. Museum of Art, Los Angeles (1968).

Selected Bibliography

This list of suggested further reading is limited to books readily available in English, and includes works cited in the Introduction. Most of these books contain bibliographies on individual artists. An asterisk indicates that the book is available in a paperback edition.

I. GENERAL SURVEYS

Kenneth Clark. *Civilisation*. New York: Harper and Row (1970)*

William Fleming. *Arts and Ideas*. New York: Holt, Rinehart and Winston (1963)

Ernst H. Gombrich. *The Story of Art*. London: Phaidon (1954)*

Arnold Hauser. *The Social History of Art*. New York: Knopf (1951)*

H. W. Janson. *History of Art*. New York: Abrams (1964)

II. SURVEYS OF FRENCH ART

Germain Bazin. *Baroque and Rococo*. New York: Praeger (1964)*

Anthony Blunt. *Art and Architecture in France, 1500 to 1700*. Baltimore: Penguin (1953)

W. G. Kalnein and M. Levy. *Art and Architecture of the 18th Century in France*. Baltimore: Penguin (1973)

Edward Lucie-Smith. *Concise History of French Painting from 1350 to the Present*. New York: Praeger (1971)*

Gerd Muehsam. *French Painters and Paintings from the 14th Century to Post-Impressionism*. New York: Ungar (1970)

Arno Schonberger and Haldor Soehner. *The Rococo Age: Art and Civilization of the 18th Century*. New York: McGraw-Hill (1960)

Jacques Thuillier and Albert Châtelet. *French Painting from Le Nain to Fragonard*. Geneva: Skira (1964)

III. SURVEYS OF 19TH CENTURY ART

Albert Boime. *The Academy and French Painting in the 19th Century*. London: Phaidon (1970)

John Canaday. *Mainstreams of Modern Art*. Englewood Cliffs: Prentice-Hall (1959)

T. J. Clark. *The Absolute Bourgeois: Artists and Politics in France, 1848-1851*. Greenwich: New York Graphic Society (1973)

Walter Friedlaender. *David to Delacroix*. Cambridge: Harvard University Press (1952)

George Heard Hamilton. *19th and 20th Century Art*. Englewood Cliffs: Prentice Hall, and New York: Abrams (1970)

George Heard Hamilton. *Painting and Sculpture in Europe, 1880-1940*. Baltimore: Penguin (1967)

Robert L. Herbert. *Barbizon Revisited*. Boston: Museum of Fine Arts (1962)*

Werner Hofmann. *Turning Points in 20th-Century Art: 1890-1917*. New York: Braziller (1969)

Jean Leymarie. *French Painting from David to Seurat*. Geneva: Skira (1959)

Linda Nochlin. *Realism*. Baltimore: Penguin (1971)*

Phoebe Pool. *Impressionism*. New York: Praeger (1967)*

Maurice Raynal. *From Baudelaire to Bonnard*. Geneva: Skira (1949)

John Rewald. *The History of Impressionism*. New York: Museum of Modern Art (1961)

John Rewald. *Post-Impressionism: From Van Gogh to Gauguin*. New York: Museum of Modern Art (1962)

STAFF

Administration

IAN McKIBBIN WHITE, *Director of Museums*
F. LANIER GRAHAM, *Vice-Director for Collections and Exhibitions, Chief Curator*
THOMAS K. SELIGMAN, *Vice-Director for Education*
DANIEL FRIEDMAN, *Vice-Director for Operations and Personnel*
MARIE S. JENSEN, *Executive Secretary to the Boards of Trustees*
WILLIAM J. GRAVESMILL, *Administrative Associate*
THOMAS L. DIBBLEE, *Administrative Assistant for Development*
EARL ANDERSON, NANCY ELSNER, *Assistants to the Director*

Curatorial Division

PAINTING AND SCULPTURE

F. LANIER GRAHAM, *Curator in Charge*
WILLIAM H. ELSNER, *Associate Curator*
WANDA M. CORN, *Visiting Curator*
TERI OIKAWA-PICANTE, *Assistant Conservator*
LYNDA C. KEFAUVER, *Curatorial Assistant*

DECORATIVE ARTS

D. GRAEME KEITH, *Curator in Charge*
GENE MUNSCH, *Conservator*
ANNA BENNETT, *Research Assistant*

PRINTS AND DRAWINGS

(Achenbach Foundation for Graphic Arts)
FENTON KASTNER, *Associate Curator in Charge*
PHYLLIS HATTIS, *Visiting Curator*
DALE MUNDAY, *Curatorial Assistant*

AFRICA, OCEANIA AND THE AMERICAS

THOMAS K. SELIGMAN, *Curator in Charge*
KATHLEEN BERRIN, *Curatorial Assistant*
JUDITH REIS, *Curatorial Assistant*

EXHIBITIONS

THOMAS H. GARVER, *Curator in Charge*
ROYAL A. BASICH, *Exhibition Designer*
MELVYN SPRENGER, *Chief Preparator*
JAMES MEDLEY, *Photographer*

Operational Division

ACCOUNTING

MARIE S. JENSEN, *Comptroller*
DELORES MALONE, *Accountant*
IRENE CASHMAN, *Recorder*
PATRICIA PIERCE, *Payroll Supervisor*

REGISTRATION

FREDERIC P. SNOWDEN, *Registrar*
JANET HEATH, *Assistant Registrar*
HARRY FUGL, *Registration Assistant*

SUPERINTENDENCE

SAL PRIOLO,
Coordinator of Museum Services
JOHN CULLEN,
Chief Engineer

Educational Division

INTERPRETATION

THOMAS K. SELIGMAN, *Curator in Charge*
CHARLES MILLS, *Assistant Curator*

PROGRAM

WILLIAM J. GRAVESMILL, *Curator in Charge*
CHARLES LONG, *Public Relations*

ART SCHOOL

ELSA CAMERON, *Curator in Charge*
RICHARD FONG, *Assistant Curator*
MEGUMI SHIMIZU, *Curatorial Assistant*
JAMES STEVENSON, *Curatorial Assistant*

LIBRARY

JANE NELSON, *Librarian*